"Captured perfectly. Morgan's words dart directly to the heart-strings. Literary configurations forever meant to be and yet coming to fruition in real time. Her book is a life's work coming together in its right timing, as it should. Her language is modern and famil-iar, laced with wisdom beyond her years." - Triana Montserrat

"After reading Morgan's beautiful journey, I realized my need to unravel the patriarchy within my own life. I connected so much with how Morgan was brought up and that desire to be PER-FECT! Since reading this, I have seen how I people please and make decisions which I believe would make everyone else around me happy rather than looking deeply into what *I* want. This chaotic way of living has caused so much emotional distress that I too am unraveling the bullshit and seeking help through EMDR. We can live a happy, joyous and free life and I am so grateful to Morgan for encouraging this next chapter in my life." - Breezy Nowlan

"Absolutely hooked! Felt like I was on an emotional journey with her, the excitement, the passion, the pain. I want to know every-thing that has happened!!" - Julia Badrya

"I believe the best reading material involves transparency. This book really helps me get to know myself and the author. Connect-ing with so much of the material, I couldn't help but feel under-stood. The authenticity and transparency of Morgan's memoir is empowering and magical!" - Brooke T. McMillin

"As someone who has been on a long journey of self discovery, this book gives a new perspective and understanding of many of the questions I've been asking myself and the universe. It is incredibly raw, honest and eye-opening! A true page turner that incites an emotional response with every page, and I loved every minute. I don't think there is anyone that wouldn't benefit from reading this book." - Liz Smith

"Morgan shares her compelling life journey with readers and brings us into her experiences. She creates opportunities for us to reflect on our own lives and revel in our own personal growth. Morgan's story is one many women can relate to and grow from." - Kellie O'Neill

"Unravel the Bullsh*t touched me on a soul level. For me, reading this book was like I was sitting in the passenger seat next to Morgan the whole ride through her journey. I laughed with her, I cried with her, I held on tight through every twist and turn with her and most importantly, I grew with her. I have the universal blessing of knowing Morgan personally so there were times during the book that I felt her pain, her strength and her triumph. Morgan's journey made me want to do better, to be better and live better. She truly shares so much of her heart and soul with us in this book and I'm so incredibly grateful that she will be able to reach so many others with her platform! Everyone deserves a little sprinkle of Morgan in their life and I believe this book is only the beginning of what the universe has in store for her and us because when you get to the last page, I guarantee you'll be asking for more! So dive in head first friends! You're in for the journey of a lifetime!" - Kelly Wiley White

Unravel the Bullsh*t

Unravel the Bullsh*t

MORGAN CHONIS

Morgan Chonis

The author of this book does not dispense medical advice or prescribe the use of any technique as a form of treatment for physical, emotional, or medical problems without the advice of a physician, either directly or indirectly. The intent of the author is only to offer information of a general nature to help you in your quest for emotional and spiritual well-being. In the event you use any of the information in this book for yourself, the author assumes no responsibility for your actions.

www.MorganChonis.com
Cover Design: Howie's Design
Cover Photo: @stephanysmithhair
Developmental Editor: Carrie Severson
Copy Editor: AmmaEdits.com
QC, VA + Emotional Support: ChelseaAnna.com
Audiobook: Costa Mesa Recording Studios

First Printing, 2021
ISBN 978-1-7378502-0-5 (paperback)
ISBN 978-1-7378502-1-2 (epub ebook)
ISBN 978-1-7378502-2-9 (audiobook)

TO THE FEMININE WHO HIDES THEIR WEIRDNESS +
THEIR FIRE IN EXCHANGE FOR PERFECTION.

TO THE MASCULINE WHO HIDES THEIR EMOTION +
THEIR PASSION BECAUSE THEY HAVE BEEN TOLD IT IS
WRONG.

I SEE YOU.
I LOVE YOU.
THIS BOOK IS FOR YOU.

CONTENTS

CONTENTS

2

The Crumbling

CONTENTS

3

The Phoenix

4

Lessons to Get You Started

CONTENTS

Introduction

Two years before beginning to write this book, my mother attended a networking event where she heard a woman named Carrie speak. Carrie was the owner of a publishing house that publishes women authors and stories with strong female leads. Knowing that I've always wanted to write a book, my mom connected me to Carrie on social media.

Years went by with no contact between us until one day, mid-global pandemic, my mother tagged me in one of Carrie's posts. That same day, I had received a private message from Carrie inquiring about my ambitions of publishing a book. I told her that I was certain at least three books were wanting to be birthed through me and that I've always been told one of my greatest gifts is my writing. I shared with her the plethora of content just sitting in the notes section of my phone, and the impending doom of imposter syndrome that continued to sweep over me as I processed through the work of beginning to express my voice with my coaches and therapists.

"Hi, Morgan!" Carrie responded. "I hear and see all of this! I get the imposter syndrome too. I've been writing for the masses for 20+ years and spent a lot of time helping other people write their stories. It is something I still do before we publish books, so if I can help get one book out of the phone and onto paper, and into a publishing pipe, let me know! I'd be happy to talk. Sending you great big waves of love!"

Exactly one month later, while home for the holidays in Tucson, I was sitting in my morning meditation, comfortably settled into my meditation pillow, when the little voice of my soul chimed in. "Call Carrie," I heard the voice say from the soft edges of my consciousness. I redirected myself back to my breathing and continued with my meditation. The following day, while deep again in meditation, I heard the voice again. "Call Carrie," it said to my consciousness. I heard the words and continued my meditation. Again on the third day, in my usual morning meditation, from the edges of consciousness came a very familiar voice. "Call Carrie!" I acknowledged then that I would in fact call Carrie and continued with my meditation.

Right after I completed my morning routine and got ready for the day, I messaged Carrie on social media to let her know about the clear nudges in my meditations. I then asked her if we could schedule a time to speak. She was available that very afternoon.

From the moment we began speaking, I felt like we were old friends. She spoke my language and was a beautifully spiritual being. As I began to share about my calling to write, and she shared about experiences she had in mind for me, I was certain within moments of meeting her that she was my person. We continued to talk on my drive home, and by the time I arrived back at my mom's house, we had gotten to the finer details of the agreement. I knew immediately within my body that this was a full-body 'fuck yes' decision! Before I could even get out of my car, I had hired Carrie to be my writing coach and developmental editor. I was elated!

After deciding the next steps, we hung up the phone and I gazed out of my windshield and burst into tears. These were not like any tears I had cried before. These tears were the result of feeling so damn proud of myself for taking such aligned action for my future!

This book is the physical manifestation of that action.

The Intention of This Book

As we transition into the Age of Aquarius[1], it is my deepest intention that this book is a tool to reawaken the light within all of its readers. My intention is for its words to meet you exactly where you are, and to ignite the fire of willingness for deeper healing. Every word in this book has been written and infused with Reiki energy, and I intend that the energy within these pages will bless you with energy healing for your highest good. As you turn each page, may you feel lovingly supported and comforted as you discover the truths of your soul, and let the warm energy of my words wrap you in a cozy blanket of compassion and love.

The theories discussed in these pages are based on my personal experiences as a white woman raised in the United States. While every attempt to remain inclusive has been taken, I am humbly aware of my privilege to even share these experiences and write this book. All opinions shared here are done to the best of my ability with the current knowledge and experiences that are solely my own.

I intend to share my experience, strength, and hope with others, so that they may find the mirror they need to continue their path to a better understanding of themselves. No opinions disclosed here are deemed as universal ultimate truths.

Throughout this book, you will see that it is my deepest hope and desire that you challenge everything you have ever been taught and shown. Challenge every mainstream conditioning, every concept of truth, every theory that resonates or triggers the fuck out of you. If my words resonate with you, that is amazing! I hope they guide you on your path to discovering *your* truth. If my words trigger you, that is amazing! I hope they guide you on your path to discovering *your* truth.

How to Read This Book

There may be topics discussed in this book that create feelings of resonance and resistance within you. That is okay! I will encourage you to begin with an open mind and to make note of those moments of resistance. Notice what creates feelings of truth and expansion within you.

Throughout this book, there will be references to topics of a Higher Power. I am in no way suggesting that there is a certain belief, religion, or spiritual preference needed to read this book. At no point will I suggest that there is a correct version of a Higher Power that you should ascribe to. In fact, I encourage you to find what works best for you.

In this book, I use terms such as Universe, Source, and Higher Power to describe the power greater than myself that I believe in. If these terms do not feel agreeable with you, please feel free to substitute them with whatever you deem to be a better fit, be it God, Heavenly Father, the Ocean, or your Blended Nonfat Sugar-free Vanilla frap-a-latte-chino, they all work just the same. Take what you like and leave the rest.

Make this book your own. Highlight, underline, make notes in the margins. This is not the type of book that you give to your bestie after you have finished reading it. This is the type of book that is so juicy and created just for you that you never dare part with it. Instead, dropship your bestie one as a surprise gift with a note that says, "You're welcome!"

Throughout the book, you will find self-reflection opportunities. These are journal prompts meant to guide you as you begin reflecting on your own life. You can use the prompts as you go or read the book in its entirety and then come back to them at the end. Whichever feels best for you is perfect, but I highly encourage you to gift yourself the opportunity to complete these self-reflection prompts.

1

The Conditioning

My Inner Child Experience

On a seemingly ordinary Friday, I jumped on my weekly Ayurveda[2] check-in session with my practitioner, Rebecca, and, as we'd done during most sessions for the last seventeen weeks, we discussed how my morning routine had been for the past week. We discussed how I did with the new nutritional updates, status of my nighttime routine, examination of my tongue, what my elimination had been like, all usual checks for our Friday morning conversations. At one point, Rebecca warmly drew my attention to one element that had been a point of contention for some time. Even while excelling in many areas, it had become clear that I had some resistance to taking my herbs.

Rebecca asked me, "Why do you suspect that is?"

I rustled through a few responses that could have been valid, but they didn't feel like truth within my body. Staring past my computer monitor for who-knows-how-long, I finally mustered, "I am not sure."

"It feels like it is something deeper," Rebecca intuitively shares.

"Mmm," I nodded.

"Can you feel in your body where you feel this resistance?" Rebecca asked.

I closed my eyes and inhaled deeply into my body. The audible depth of this first breath alluded to a high likelihood that I had probably not been breathing while staring off into the thought proces-sor of my brain until now. I continued this breath deep into my belly and allowed myself to sink into my body. My awareness was immediately drawn into my chest. My heart center was activated in a seemingly unpleasant way, and I instantly knew that we had hit the jackpot. Watching me melt into my heart center, Rebecca sat warmly, holding space for me to process what I was feeling. That feeling in my chest was familiar. It was painful. It was physical.

I jumbled through some thoughts, feeling into my body even deeper. As the next inhale reached the pits of my belly, I muttered, "There is a little girl in there with a big attitude. She has this sass, and she's proclaiming, 'You're not gonna *tell me* what to do!'" I recog-nized her instantly. She was very familiar indeed. The physical pain in my chest was coming from within my ribcage, and it grew. As I look back at Rebecca, a tender example of what it looks like to hold space for a vulnerable experience, she asked me if she may send me Reiki while I continued exploring. Agreeing graciously, I closed my eyes and sank even deeper into my body.

I connected again with the tiny girl inside my chest, the scowl on her face undeniable. I breathed deeply and began to examine her. Her hip was cocked ajar, her eyes piercing, her energetic walls sky-rocketing. She was guarded and projecting an undeniable shell of disdain. As I drew another breath deep into my belly, I transitioned from examining to analyzing.

- **Why does she seem so familiar?** She is a tiny, young version of me. No question there.
- **Why is she so guarded?** She is protecting herself.
- **Is she threatening to me?** No. She seems fragile and appears to be projecting this shell of disdain as a response to feeling threatened herself.

- **What did I do to threaten her?** I'd been working with Rebecca to place gradual structure and habits in place to evolve my vitality.
- **I'd been making great progress, why are we having such an issue here?** She is clawing on for dear life, trying to maintain some sense of control and independence.

Bingo! I am threatening two of her basic human needs. While the 2021 version of Morgan feels like these changes, structure, and habits are all evolving quite slowly and pleasantly, tiny Morgan is grasping at straws trying to maintain a sense of control and normalcy. With each passing week, I threaten her certainty and her significance.

I sighed in relief.

I now understood. That rage inside of her was the result of a deep-rooted pattern I had become aware of, in myself, just two years ago. Up until then, my primary core values[3] had been certainty and significance. Her rage was valid. I completely understood.

Rebecca gently gestured, "What would grownup Morgan like to say to young Morgan?"

With my eyes still closed, my voice dropped to a compassionate tone, "I am not here to hurt you. I hear you. I see you. I understand your rage. Although it may feel that way, I am not a threat. I am doing this work for us!"

The rage she was feeling was a response triggered by her "fight, flight, or freeze" mechanisms in her homo-sapien brain which, through no fault of her own, had not evolved much in the last thirty thousand years. Tiny Morgan's brain was doing *exactly* what it had been trained to do. She felt threatened by an external source, which is really just a thought that she had determined, by the grace of her frontal lobe, to be ultimately true. Therefore tiny Morgan was certain she was under attack, thus fight or flight mode had been activated! And she had chosen to fight.

Now that we had analyzed the situation with tiny Morgan, I wondered if we had reached a conclusion to the point of solving this resistance. I brought my attention back to my screen where Rebecca was still giving me Reiki, and I shared, "That is all valid, but I don't know. It just feels like that isn't deep enough to solve what is going on here. I don't believe that this can be the full reason for this much resistance." Rebecca smiled softly and continued to deliver Reiki. I sat back in my chair, preparing to dive in again.

As I dropped back into my body, I headed straight for the space within my ribcage where I knew tiny Morgan to be. I was struck as I descended to her. I was so closely connected with her before that I had not even noticed the surroundings. The pain in my chest ignited again. I met her gaze as I slowly transcended upon a cage. The pain grew.

I didn't speak straight away, I merely took it all in. Tiny Morgan stands at attention within a metal cage. It is a decent amount larger than she is, perhaps why I did not notice it before, but about the size of a Victorian bird cage. I feel very taken aback that I did not notice this before. I find myself on my knees before her. I tell her again, "I am not here to hurt you. I am doing this for us."

She scoffed, "You've said that before."

Stumbling to collect my words, I told her, "I promise you; this is all for our good."

"Yea, yea!" she says, "I know that is what *you* believe, but that is not the truth. We do this all the time." I softened and allowed her to continue. "Time and time again you make these promises to yourself and then like clockwork, POOF! Gone."

I sat back onto my feet; she is not wrong. So much of the cleaning up the wreckage of my past had been in restoring my integrity out in the world. My word is so valuable to me, but I had been out of integrity for so long that it had taken a lot of work to begin forgiving myself. That is the funny part about making amends with another person for my behavior; even if they forgive me, I have to be willing to forgive myself. Not forgiving myself for the wreckage I have caused is like choosing to still drink the poison the other person has already told me I no longer have to drink. It makes absolutely no logical sense but, for an alcoholic like me, lessons tend to penetrate, sometimes quickly, sometimes slowly. I often tread in the "sometimes slowly" side of these lessons.

"This isn't new. This has been going on for generations!" Tiny Morgan explains, "We are constantly being told 'This is for your own good.' or 'Trust me, it's safe' blah blah blah!"

Oh. My eyes softened to her. The pain in my chest was becoming physically unbearable. Again, she was not wrong.

"Come around here with your friendly face on, trying to tell me what is best for me! You don't know me!" The radius of rage circling her is dense. "And heaven forbid I stand up for myself, Oh no! I'll be hung by a noose or stoned again!"

Oh, this is way deeper than just her and me.

"May as well just burn me at the stake for being a girl too!" she rages.

The pain in my chest was now completely unbearable. I feel as though someone is taking a wooden baseball bat to the insides of my ribcage. This pain and rage feel as though it could explode from within me at any given moment. I opened my eyes and saw Rebecca listening intently, still delivering Reiki. She gave me a soft nod. As I pursed my lips and returned the nod, I felt the tears beginning to swell in my eyes. This rage was so much deeper. My heart broke.

At that moment I saw it all so clearly. I softly thanked Rebecca as I began to weep relentlessly. I closed my eyes again, knowing that the only way to properly process through this was *through*. I went back in for more.

"Oh, sweet girl," I told her, "This is not your fault. This is not your fault at all." She continued to keep my gaze.

"This rage you are feeling is generations upon generations of the repressed feminine. We come from a lineage connected to it all!" Her gaze grows curious.

"Womxn[4] have been persecuted, oppressed, victimized, exiled, burned, stoned, raped, and shamed for being feminine for millennia. It is heartbreaking and infuriating, but this is the truth. This rage that you feel inside is the same rage that burned inside millions of womxn before us. This is the fire woven throughout all of womxnkind and you, sweet girl, are brave enough to feel it all!" There was a crack in her shell. I reached for her hands as she began to soften, she allowed me to stay. I did.

"Where I come from, there are womxn who look nothing like me who are also experiencing this rage inside of them. Those who identify as feminine are ridiculed and harassed every single day in our world. It is horrendous and it must stop. The patriarchy is falling, and we are all, together, paving the way for the future. The changes we seek are not immediate, but as you feel the decades of flames within you, we must break the chain!" I had her full attention now, her hands still wrapped within mine.

"If we do this work together, you and me, we can break this chain in our lineage. We can create a different path for those who will come behind us. Nothing will change if nothing changes!" Her eyes began to swell, and I softly held her tighter.

Connecting deeply within her eyes, I told her, "I need you. I need you to be with me. I cannot do this without you. We have to do this together!"

"Please," I sobbed, "I cannot do this without you. We have to do this together."

Through the stream running down her face, she nods. Through the uncontrollable sobs, I began to beam. Before she could even speak, I wrapped her entire body within mine. "I love you so much," I whispered to the top of her head. "I love you so much, and I vow from this moment forward to always protect you and to do everything in my power to never let you feel this way again." She didn't move from within my embrace. We just sobbed.

Separately and together, we just sobbed.

Finding breath beginning to make its way back into my body, I felt the tension in my back begin to soften. I slowly gasped for more. With each cleansing breath, I found myself more into my body. I was coming back into the chair at my desk, as the pain began to melt away from my chest. Noticing that both of my hands were still on my heart, I had turned on my Reiki for myself when we began as well, I slowly sank deeper into my chair. After a few more slow, full belly deep cleansing breaths, I softly began to blink my eyes open.

Rebecca sat before me, silently, still holding space for me. I softened my gaze and began to turn up a smile at her. I think to myself, "This is such a beautiful example of the type of people I am available for in my life." I sighed, and she nods, turning off her Reiki. That was intense.

"That was incredibly brave of you," Rebecca says to me. My heart melted; it is true. That was an incredibly courageous act of 'doing the work' that was completely unexpected within our session together.

"It's completely different now," I began to share. "Making proclamations for myself because it feels good now doesn't work for me anymore. This is serious now. That vow I made to her is very serious to me. Incredibly serious to me!" I began to feel the shift that had taken place within my body. The cracking rib cage had subsided, and

I felt a sense of honor and trust that had been bestowed upon me. I felt a sense of calm come over me, clear that all of the feelings inside me had been validated but could now be used for good. Tiny Morgan and I could step forward each day together to make more positive and aligned choices, not only for us but for all who will come tomorrow.

Today, I am reminded that this is a one-day-at-a-time program, a daily reprieve contingent on the maintenance of my spiritual condition. Just for today, together we will break the chain.

This rage is in no way limited to women who bleed. These energetic cords run deep within lineages of all womxn who identify as feminine, who allow their wild to be seen, heard, loved, or felt. To those womxn I say, I love you. I see you.

Healing Tool: Every morning for a week, look yourself in the eye and repeat this short mantra at least five times in a row. Looking yourself in the eye, speak it out loud.

"I love you. I'm sorry. Please forgive me. Thank you."

Repeat.

This mantra is called Ho'oponopono. It is a Hawaiian ritual for forgiveness, and I have seen it mend marriages certain of divorce in a matter of moments. I have also practiced this mirror work myself and found incredibly powerful results. If you are beginning to sweat at the thought of even looking yourself in the eye, I tell you this:

"I love you so much. That little child inside of you is so afraid. Please be brave for them. We need you."

If you can receive the above, which I deliver from the depths of my heart to you, I encourage you to challenge yourself to 30 days of Ho'oponopono. I would not steer you wrongly on this one. I will be honest, this may be very uncomfortable in the beginning, but hold on to your ass and do it anyway. Tiny Morgan recognizes the Tiny You and is telling you to be brave. We love you.

2

Soul Agreements

Stepping out of the victim mindset[5] has been one of the most challenging lessons for me to master thus far in my spiritual journey. The disease of addiction taught me that the core of my natural thoughts is selfish and self-centered, and by working on a 12-Step program, I have learned to not let those thoughts control my actions. Of course, some days are better than others. Luckily, I have been trained to strive for progress, not perfection. One of my favorite mantras to live outside of a victim-dominated mindset is, "Life is happening FOR me, not to me."

Remaining in this truth allowed me to put on a new pair of glasses in every area of my life, and it can do the same for you. To truly embody this mindset, one thing is absolutely required - willingness. And for any change to occur, we must be willing to see things differently. The true embodiment of a victimless mindset is when we accept that every experience we have had, and will ever have, is happening *for* us.

This gets interesting when we begin examining our relationships with others. Before incarnating on Earth in this lifetime, my soul was at a cocktail party out in the universe somewhere, mingling with all the other souls, chit-chatting about the experiences we wanted to have in this incarnation on Earth, and what lessons we needed to have this time around.

This other soul said to me, "Hey! How would you like to have this super sacred bond with me, I'll teach you everything I know, and then just when you think you are figuring life all out, I am going to break your heart in a way that you never see coming?"

"Sounds great," I said. We shook hands and agreed to connect again on Earth. That soul would be my Father.

My soul mingled around some more and met this vivacious soul. "Hey! How would you like to fall in love and explore your sexual pleasures in a way you've never done before?"

"Sounds great," I said.

"Great! We will fall in love, build an empire and then I'm going to quietly screw you over, so you have to learn how to stand up to bullies."

"Cool! I want to learn to stand up to bullies in this life," I said. We shook hands and agreed to connect again on Earth. That soul would be one of my business partners.

Excited about the agreements that are being made, my soul continued to mingle around at the party.

"Hey! How would you like to redefine your relationship with your Higher Power?" another soul asked.

"Oh yes! I want to deepen my connection with my Higher Power in this incarnation," I agreed.

"Great," they said, "I am going to sweep you off your feet, flip your world on its head, be your biggest cheerleader, stimulate you into other dimensions until you place me on the highest pedestal in your life. Then we are going to ride this intense entanglement together until you learn who is in control of your life."

"Sounds exhilarating, I'm in!" We shook hands and that soul became one of my greatest loves.

Each soul continued around the party meeting all the other souls they needed to meet, creating soul agreements for their experiences and lessons together, and so it was.

We will meet some souls here on Earth, whom we might feel like we've known before, others will be more casual encounters that may seem insignificant at first. But remember that our soul agreements are the contracts that we made before incarnating into this human experience. And it is our job as we live through the schoolhouse of life, to uncover the lessons that we are here to learn from them.

Whatever your personal beliefs about past lives and incarnations may be, that is perfect. I am not here to tell you that any belief you have, religious or spiritual, is correct or incorrect. I believe that every one of us is here to learn our own unique set of lessons, through our own unique set of experiences.

And I stand firm in the belief that every experience I have in this lifetime is happening for me, not to me. It is in these moments that I can look to my greatest enemies and remember that we made soul agreements to share these experiences and that I am truly separate from the victimhood of my ego. However the experiences turned out, however intense they may have felt, however devastating they may have seemed, they were all happening for me. I agreed to incarnate here on Earth, at this time in history, to have these experiences.

To every soul who ever wronged me, thank you.

To every soul who ever loved me, thank you.

To every soul who held up a mirror for me to grow, thank you.

And to every soul yet to grace my path, I look forward to our experience together. I look forward to what you will teach me. I look forward to moving forward in this human experience with a brand-new pair of glasses.

3

Lessons from Losing My Dad

My dad left us a legacy of love, and a business of compassion and loyalty. He left us an empire not built on money, but on the promise that we would never go hungry. An empire that provided safety for all the kindred souls who couldn't find that sovereignty in their own homes. He guided broken spirits and provided rehab for their broken wings. He supported the underdogs, and he always rolled with the little guys.

He built an empire on integrity and soul, and he secured it with thumbtacks and number two pencils. He built everything by hand, one day at a time. He nurtured with humor and mentored with compassion. He built a legacy of perfect harmony, a perfect balance of healed masculine and the divine feminine. He was a true hu(man).

After the unexpected passing of my father just days before his sixtieth birthday, I sat reflecting on my life and how I would carry on his legacy, and I wrote this poem:

SANDCASTLES

I BUILT A SUCCESSFUL SANDCASTLE OUT OF MY WOUNDED MASCU-
LINE.

| 19 |

I DIDN'T KNOW IT WAS WOUNDED BECAUSE I PERFECTLY POR-
TRAYED THE VERSION OF A "BOSS BITCH" THE PATRIARCHY REQUIRED
OF ME.
THEY DON'T TELL YOU THAT IT'S WOUNDED BECAUSE THEY DON'T
KNOW.
THEY ARE THE PATRIARCHY.
THEY TOO ARE A REFLECTION OF WOUNDED MASCULINE.
THEY DON'T KNOW WHAT THEY DON'T KNOW.

I HAVE SYMPATHY FOR THEM BECAUSE THEY DON'T KNOW.
THAT'S THE THING ABOUT NOT KNOWING, WE WILL DO EVERY-
THING IN OUR POWER TO SILENCE THE NUDGES, THE WARNINGS, THE
DISCOMFORT.
WE DRINK.
WE USE.
WE FUCK.
WE EAT.
WE NUMB.

WE NUMB THE FIRE OF OUR SOUL THAT IS SCREAMING AT US TO
OPEN OUR EYES.
WE DEVELOP ANXIETY, DEPRESSION, DIS-EASE.
WE NUMB HARDER.

LIKE THERE IS A BADGE OF HONOR STATING, "I NUMB SO HARD
THAT NO ONE WILL EVER KNOW I'M DYING INSIDE BECAUSE I'M PRO-
JECTING THIS PATRIARCHAL REFLECTION OF ALL THE REQUIRED BE-
HAVIORS FOR SUCCESS! I AM SUCCESSFUL BECAUSE I AM NUMBING
SO HARD!"

THAT IS THE BADGE OF HONOR THAT THE PATRIARCHAL PARTICI-
PATION TROPHY WILL WEAR.

THE THING ABOUT THE SUCCESSFUL SANDCASTLES,
THEY ARE BUILT COMPLETELY OUT OF HOPES + DREAMS
GLUED TOGETHER BY PRIDE AND EGO.

ON THE SURFACE, THESE SANDCASTLES LOOK STRONG
WELL-MANICURED
SAFELY SURROUNDED BY THEIR MOATS AND GATORS.

EVERY NEW ADDITION TO THE SANDCASTLE COSTS A PORTION OF
YOUR SOUL.
YOUR SOUL IS GROUND INTO PRIDE AND EGO AND SHOVED BE-
TWEEN THOUSANDS OF LITTLE GRAINS OF SAND, MOLDED, AND
FORMED INTO THE NEWEST WING OF YOUR SHINY CASTLE.

THE GOAL OF EVERY SUCCESSFUL SANDCASTLE IS "MORE."
MORE TOWERS.
MORE DANGER PLACED WITHIN THE MOAT.
MORE THINGS.
MORE STUFF.
MORE. MORE. MORE.

SOME SANDCASTLE BUILDERS GET SO ADDICTED TO "MORE" THAT
THEY ARE STILL ADDING MORE BEFORE THEY'VE EVEN REALIZED THEY
ARE COMPLETELY OUT OF PIECES OF THEIR SOUL TO SELL!

THIS, HOWEVER, DOES NOT STOP THE CASE OF THE MORES.

THIS CASE OF THE MORES INITIATES THE SECOND PHASE OF
SANDCASTLE OWNERSHIP,
SKILLED NEGOTIATION.

WE BEGIN TO DRIP SMALL DROPLETS OF HONEY
IN FRONT OF THE LINE OF ANTS DOWN THE ROAD.

WE GIVE THEM A LITTLE TASTE OF OUR HONEY
AND SLOWLY BACK TOWARDS OUR SANDCASTLE
LEAVING LITTLE DROPLETS OF THIS SWEET NECTAR ALONG OUR
PATH.

THEY FOLLOW.
THEY LOVE THIS NECTAR.
THIS IS THE SWEETEST HONEY THEY HAVE EVER TASTED.

WE EXPLAIN WE HAVE MORE HONEY FOR THEM.
THE LITTLE ANTS REJOICE IN THEIR GOOD FORTUNE!
WE CROSS BACK INTO OUR SANDCASTLES
AND INVITE THE SEDUCED ANTS ACROSS OUR DRAWBRIDGE
OVER THE MOAT OF FIRE BREATHING GATORS
AND INTO THE SAFETY OF OUR CASTLE WALLS.

LOOKING AT US WITH BEAMING EYES,
THE ANTS ASK FOR MORE HONEY.
WE DRIP ONE DROP.
THEY SCURRY TO SHARE BUT A LICK.

THE ANTS FIND THEMSELVES TRAMPLING OVER EACH OTHER
ONLY TO FIND THE HONEY GONE BEFORE THE DUST SETTLES BE-
FORE THEM.

THEY LOOK TO US.

WE ASSURE THEM THERE IS MORE HONEY.

AT THIS MOMENT, ALL ANTS STAND AT ATTENTION.

"BUT THERE IS JUST ONE LITTLE THING," WE SPEAK GINGERLY TO
THE ANTS.

"JUST ONE LITTLE THING I NEED YOU TO DO BEFORE I CAN GIVE
YOU MORE HONEY."

"ANYTHING!" THEY SCURRY WILLINGLY TO OUR FEET.

"YOU SEE," WE SAY,

"THERE IS A NEW WING OF MY SANDCASTLE THAT MUST BE COM-
PLETED

BEFORE DUSK ARRIVES WITH THE EVENING RAIN."

THE ANTS DELIGHT WITH THIS REQUEST,

AS THEY ARE SKILLED LABORERS TOGETHER.

"WE CAN COMPLETE YOUR SANDCASTLE
IN EXCHANGE FOR MORE HONEY!
NO PROBLEM!"

THE ANTS SCURRY OFF INTO FORMATION.

NO SOUL SOLD IN EXCHANGE FOR THE NEW ADDITION TO OUR
SANDCASTLE.

THIS NECTAR OF THE GODS TASTES SO GOOD

WHEN WATCHING OUR CASTLE BEING BUILT BY THE HAND OF AN-
OTHER.

THE ANTS DID NOT HAVE TO SELL THEIR SOUL TO BUILD THE NEW
WING OF THE SANDCASTLE.
THE ANTS PLAYED WILLINGLY IN MUCH ANTICIPATION OF REWARD.

THIS IS THE BUSINESS MODEL OF OUR PRIZED PATRIARCHY.
WE, THE OWNERS OF THE SANDCASTLE,
WILL EAT THE PROMISED HONEY
WHILE WATCHING THE EAGER ANTS BUILD INTO DAYS END.

THIS IS A PROJECTION OF WOUNDED MASCULINE.
THIS IS THE FOUNDATION OF OUR SUCCESSFUL SANDCASTLES.

I HAD A BEAUTIFUL SANDCASTLE.
MY FAMILY WAS PROUD.
SOCIETY TOLD ME I WAS SUCCESSFUL.
OTHERS PEERED ENVIOUSLY AT HOW SHINY MY SANDCASTLE WAS.
I LIKED MY SANDCASTLE.
I LIKED THE TASTE OF THE SWEET NECTAR.
I REALLY LIKED THE CASE OF THE MORES.
MORE WAS FUN!
MORE WAS SEXY!

I WOULD WAKE EACH MORNING AND DRAW THE CURTAINS FROM
MY TOWER.
I WOULD DRESS FOR THE DAY AND WALK TO MY FAVORITE BAKER.
I WOULD COLLECT MY BREAD AND MY BREWED COURAGE.

IN THE TWENTY-FIVE YARDS FROM THE TOWER TO MY BAKER
I WOULD BEGIN TO FEEL A HEAT RISING INSIDE MY CHEST.
I WOULD LIGHT MENTHOL TO SOOTHE THE BURN.

THERE'S A UTOPIA OF PLEASURE THAT HAPPENS IN THOSE FIRST SIPS OF COURAGE AND THAT MENTHOL.

ECSTASY.

POWER.

SEX.

MY BODY REVOLTED INTO A DRY HEAVE INTO THE BUSHES BESIDE ME.

I IGNORE IT.

MMM … YES, THE SATISFACTION OF THAT MORNING COURAGE AND THAT DRAG OF MENTHOL SEX DOWN THE BACK OF MY THROAT.

THIS. THIS MOMENT RIGHT HERE.

THIS MOMENT BEFORE EVEN ARRIVING TO OTHER HUMANS, I HAVE A CHOICE TO MAKE IN SANDCASTLE-SHIP.

OPTION A) ACKNOWLEDGE THE PHYSICAL REPULSION THAT MY BODY JUST DISPLAYED

OR OPTION B) TAKE ANOTHER DRAG OF MORNING MENTHOL SEX STICK.

I WASH IT DOWN WITH STEAMY HOT COURAGE AND CONTINUE DOWN MY PATH.

THIS MOMENT. THIS DECISION RIGHT HERE!

THIS DECISION IS WHAT WINNERS ARE MADE OF.

THIS IS WHAT THE PATRIARCHY TELLS US.

THAT BITCH HAS BALLS.

THAT BITCH IS ON A MISSION.

THAT BITCH IS IN CONTROL.

UNBEKNOWNST TO ME, I GET TO WEAR THE "I NUMB SO HARD THAT NO ONE WILL EVER KNOW I'M DYING INSIDE BECAUSE I'M PROJECTING THIS PATRIARCHAL REFLECTION OF ALL THE REQUIRED BEHAVIORS FOR SUCCESS! I AM SUCCESSFUL BECAUSE I AM NUMBING SO HARD" BADGE OF HONOR FOR THE REST OF THE DAY!
I AM. FUCKING. WINNING.

BEFORE MY DAILY ROUND-UP MEETING TO START THE DAY, I FEEL NAUSEOUS AGAIN.
I LIGHT UP ANOTHER MENTHOL SEX STICK
AND INHALE IT DEEP DOWN THE BACK OF MY THROAT.
AH. MUCH BETTER.
NOW, WHERE'S MY STEAMY MUG OF COURAGE?

THIS LASTS FOR A COUPLE OF HOURS
AND THE NUDGES BEGIN TO TAP AGAIN.
THE FIRE IN THE PITS OF MY SOUL BEGINS TO RUMBLE.
I BETTER MAKE A MOVE!

I HOP ON MY LITTLE BICYCLE AND CHECK ON ALL THE WORKER ANTS.
IT IS NECESSARY TO SHOW MY IMPORTANCE,
SO THEY KNOW THEIR PROGRESS DETERMINES THE ARRIVAL OF THEIR HONEY
THAT WE'VE ALREADY EATEN.

THERE ARE SOME ANTS THAT WILL STOP WHAT THEY ARE DOING TO HONOR ME AS I FLY BY.
SWEET GESTURES AND TOKENS OF THEIR AFFECTION,
AND I AM OFF AGAIN.

I FEEL THE FIRE EXTINGUISH
AND MY SEXY SANDCASTLENESS RETURNS.

WE INDULGE IN LAVISH TASTINGS TO SATISFY OUR HARD WORK
AND ENDLESS SUPPLY OF HONEYPOTS.
NO ONE ELSE CAN SEE INSIDE THE HONEYPOTS.
THEY DON'T KNOW WHAT THEY DON'T KNOW.

I SIT UPON THE PORCH OF MY TOWER DIGESTING THE DAY,
TAKING DOWN A FEW MORE MENTHOL SEX STICKS AS I SIT IN
STILLNESS.
THE SEX STICKS BRING STILLNESS.

I AM PROUD OF MY SANDCASTLE.
I'M WILLING TO AUCTION OFF THE SOULS OF THE ANTS ANOTHER
DAY
IN ORDER TO CONTINUE BUILDING MY SANDCASTLE.

THEY DON'T KNOW WHAT THEY DON'T KNOW.

IT TAKES ANOTHER FEW SEX STICKS TO GATHER MY THOUGHTS.
I SHOWER AND RETREAT TO BED.
WHAT'S MORE THAN A SUCCESSFUL SANDCASTLE?

I HAVE NEW IDEAS FOR ADDITIONAL SANDCASTLES.
IF WE BUILD MORE SANDCASTLES
NEXT TO THIS SANDCASTLE
THEN WE HAVE AN EMPIRE.

THE GOAL OF EVERY SANDCASTLE OWNER IS TO RULE AN EMPIRE.

UNDER THE RAIN OF CLARITY, CREATIVE JUICES PUMP THROUGH
MY BLOOD.
STROKES OF GENIUS FOR EMPIRE BUILDING ARE EMERGING.
TOMORROW WE WILL BUILD MORE.

I AM GOOD AT BUILDING SANDCASTLES.
THE PATRIARCHY TAUGHT ME HOW TO BEHAVE
IN ORDER TO PLAY IN THE SANDBOX WITH THE BIG BOYS.

I DON'T KNOW WHAT I DON'T KNOW.

WHAT I DO KNOW IS THAT I AM IMPECCABLY SKILLED AT NUMBING.
"I NUMB SO HARD THAT NO ONE WILL EVER KNOW I'M DYING INSIDE
BECAUSE I'M PROJECTING THIS PATRIARCHAL REFLECTION OF ALL
THE REQUIRED BEHAVIORS FOR SUCCESS! I AM SUCCESSFUL BECAUSE
I AM NUMBING SO HARD!"

WHAT I DO KNOW IS THAT I AM IMPECCABLY SKILLED AT PROJECT-
ING.

WHAT I DO KNOW IS THAT I AM IMPECCABLY SKILLED AT CHOOSING
TO HAVE A SUCCESSFUL SANDCASTLE OVER HAVING ANY CONNEC-
TION TO THE RAGING BEASTS TRYING TO GROW INSIDE OF ME.

I AM IMPECCABLY SKILLED AT WINNING IN PATRIARCHY.
I DON'T KNOW WHAT I DON'T KNOW.

Years after having multiple sandcastles, helping others build
sandcastles, and a big shiny life of wearing my badge of honor that
said, "I can numb so hard," I received a phone call from my father.
My dad was the epitome of all things. Nothing else mattered to me

if he wasn't proud of me. And heaven forbid that I disappointed him! My dad was very proud of the sandcastles I'd built. He was even prouder when I burned it all to the ground to honor the tiny little light inside of me that was struggling to flicker through another day.

My dad was prouder of me when I began to accept my mental health.

My dad was even prouder when I ventured down the path of personal development.

My dad was even prouder when I walked away from unworthy toxic relations.

My dad was even prouder when I spent the last dime that I owned, to choose joy.

My dad was even prouder when I started to exercise my voice.

My dad was even prouder when I started to be of service to other women.

My dad was even prouder when I worked up the courage to break old patterns.

My dad was proudest when I decided to say, 'fuck the patriarchy,' and followed the path that most lights me up.

My dad watched me hand over the director's chair to a power greater than myself, who swiftly washed away the sandcastles. Poof. Gone. My ego liked the theatrics, but to my dismay, the shifts were glacial and silent most days.

Souls you can't live without. Poof. Gone.

Man of your dreams. Poof.

Rose-colored glasses. Gone.

Sitting alone in my brand-new apartment, my phone rang. I had just moved in two months prior, with the man I was ready to marry. In illusions of grandeur, there was a tiny little light inside me struggling to flicker one more day. I won't numb it, not this time. This time I choose to honor you, little, tiny light inside me. Poof. Man. Gone.

My dad is so proud of me.

My phone rang again. It was my dad. His voice was different. His voice is always a certain way: Light, funny, proud. This day my dad was different. He explained to me that he had cancer. My heart sank into my couch. I already knew. I had felt it two days earlier in our energy healing session together. It was angry. It did not like me in there playing with it. It did not want to loosen its grip on his spine. It wouldn't so much as budge, no matter how much I tried. It was very angry.

"Multiple Myeloma," he explained, "rare cancer in my blood. It's attacking my spine." He says, "I could die." That is not possible! He will be fine. He is the epitome of all things. He will obviously be fine.

He called me the next morning. I could hear the terror in his voice and the tears streaming down his face. He said, "Come be with me. Come help me get things in order. Please just come be with me." I packed a bag and was on the highway out of town in mere moments.

Exactly thirty days later. Poof. Gone.

My father built a legacy on love. He built an empire on integrity and soul.

Never again will I strive for the sandcastles of the patriarchy. With my heart shattered and snot streaming down my face, I will forever honor his legacy. I will never settle for anything less than integrity and love, for these are what unbreakable foundations are made of. And as the sandcastles of the patriarchy are washed away by the shore, I will never forget all of those mornings when my body would dramatically try to get my attention. I had it in me all along, but spoiler alert, the light was rising, and the patriarchy isn't victorious this time.

4

Daddy's Girl

I was born into a loving, middle-class home in Tucson, Arizona. My mother was a realtor, and my father owned a restaurant in town. We always had a roof over our heads, and food on the table. Being an only child until the age of 5, some of my earliest memories come from the VHS tapes and faded photo albums at my grandmother's house. I was adored by my aunts and often shared holidays with my cousin, who is only six months older than I am. I was raised in the family restaurant and had many honorary uncles who coddled and loved me. Contrary to half the population in America, my parents also remained married until my father's dying breath. All things considered, I was raised in a very positive, privileged, and loving household.

I remember being on the swing at the park with my dad as a tiny little peanut, and one of my favorite photographs in the entire world is of me in a polka dot dress pushing my dad on my tricycle, probably at the age of three. Another one of the only other memories I can recall from before my brother was born is of me standing at my bedroom window, hysterically crying while watching my dad leave the house. Being the owner of a restaurant, he was always very busy, but for some reason, this time sticks out in my memory. I have no idea where he was going, or what he was doing, but I was so distraught watching my father leave the house that day that I couldn't peel myself away from the window to go to the bathroom that I peed my pants right there on my bedroom carpet, desperately latching on to the window seal. To this day, I have no idea why that moment was so traumatic for me. My dad has always been my everything, the epitome of all things. Even surpassing his very last breath, my father is my best friend, and I am a daddy's girl through and through.

My dad was my knight in shining armor, and I was the bright twinkle in his eye. I grew up visiting him at the restaurant. I was helping him make fresh pizza dough before I could even reach the scratch table. No matter how busy he was, I was always made to feel important at the restaurant. Customers knew me, the staff loved me, and what kid doesn't love a lifetime supply of pizza!

My mother signed me up for summer cheerleading camp at the age of four. She was excited to have a girly girl just like her. Dressed in my adorable little outfit, after hours and hours of practice, we attended our first basketball game. From an outsider's perspective, this was probably stinking cute, watching a bunch of cute little girls cheering on this basketball game, but I remember it very differently. To be honest, I remember it like it was yesterday. The cheer was called "SPIRIT" and it was very simple.

"S... S-P... S-P-I-R-I-T... Spirit! Spirit!"

Although simple enough, I was so uncomfortable in this experience: the dress, the hair, the people, my spirit came out "S-P-I-T" and the whole crowd roared in laughter at the one cute little girl who messed up the SPIRIT cheer. I have no idea if the whole stadium ruptured in laughter or not, but for a tiny little four-year-old, the experience was mortifying. I am willing to bet that this was the moment when I subconsciously vowed to never be bad at anything ever again.

As my mother grew more pregnant with my brother, I was experiencing my first year of public school. I was quickly deemed to be a social butterfly and had a hard time abiding by the restrictive schedule that included nap time. Eight days after my fifth birthday, my brother was born. Caring for my new baby brother made me feel very important. And as I entered into first grade I was just as quickly deemed to be boy crazy, having had my first kiss in the reading corner of our classroom. By the third grade, I was assigned to an in-class "lunch bunch" for a group of girls who couldn't seem to get along.

I didn't understand why the other girls couldn't understand that recess would be so much more fun if they would just follow my rules for all the playground activities and which boys they were allowed to chase. But apparently, all such organizational skills got you was the bossy label and grammar school's version of lunchtime detention. I had very strong opinions that hurt other girls' feelings, so I was constantly being reprimanded to play nice and let other kids be in charge also. But their games were boring, and the boys didn't like playing with us when the other girls were in charge. So I took it upon myself to play the games the boys played because I wasn't as interested in hopscotch and hair braiding as I was in four square and wall ball. Other girls my age were more interested in making friends with each other, but I was more interested in expressing my competitive edge amongst the boys. I was not dainty like other girls my age, and I tended to vocalize my opinions very freely.

This often led to me receiving punishment responses, even though I was an excellent student and always received satisfactory remarks on my report cards. I was beginning to be taught that my socialization and fitting in with others were more important than my academics. That was until I met my fifth-grade teacher, Ms. Anderson.

Besides the Hispanic caretaker whom I spent time with, Ms. Anderson was my first teacher of color. Ms. Andy, as we adoringly called her, was the first influential adult in my life whom I recall teaching me about diversity and inclusivity. Unlike the other grade school classes I had had before, all of the students in Ms. Andy's class felt equal. There were no cliques, no cool girls, no outcasts. We were somehow all equally important. This was a pivotal point in my life because whereas I had previously often been ridiculed for my opinions and competitiveness, I distinctly remember feeling very comfortable in her classroom.

I always felt safe to be myself in Ms. Andy's class, and I even made some girl friends that year. Ms. Andy encouraged us to think for ourselves, be true to ourselves, and be comfortable standing as an individual in a room of varying characters and opinions. To this day, I still think about my gratitude to her and how that was probably one of the last times that I felt truly safe to be unapologetically myself.

5

Working at 12

I didn't understand the emphasis on socialization that occurred in grade school, and since I often found myself being ridiculed for my big personality and opinions, I took stock of my worth and attention where I felt like it mattered, to my dad. And since the best place to spend time with my dad was to hang around the pizza shop, that's where you often found me. I loved watching him work. He was in his comfort zone, and it was magical to me. From the way he scratched a pizza, to the way he leaned on the counter to talk to everyone, to the number two pencil tucked behind his ear, he just had this cool guy swagger about him. He knew everyone by name and always knew what was going on with their families. Everyone who came into the shop loved talking with him because my dad was just so cool! I remember always watching him and thinking to myself, "I've never felt that comfortable in my own skin." I wanted to be just like my dad when I grew up! He was my idol, my mentor, and my very best friend.

My dad taught me everything he knew, especially what he called his "MacGyver Skills." No matter what issues came up around the restaurant, he could fix anything. Swamp cooler went out in the middle of a summertime rush, no problem! Dad threw the ladder against the back wall and climbed up on the roof himself. The ice machine took a dump and leaked all over the floor, dad had the mop and the right kind of tape to seal the leak. A lot of the equipment in that restaurant was older than I was, and he rarely replaced a thing in over thirty years. He had a trick and a solution for everything, it just needed a little elbow grease and that magic touch.

I soaked up everything I could from him and found myself workin' the counter by the time I was twelve years old. I used to stand on a soda crate just to see the cash register, but no one was the wiser until I would jump down to grab their drinks.

"Whoa! Where'd she go?!" was a very common response from the other side of the counter. I didn't mind, I got to spend time with my dad and that's all that mattered to me. As I would be filling plastic cups with the world's most perfect crushed ice, I'd see him look over at me, stretched dough in hand, and just smile from ear to ear. He was happy having me around, and my heart was full to the brim!

I worked on the weekends and every chance I could get through middle school. The customers loved me, and I loved spending so much time with my dad. I felt important, needed, and loved. The shop was a safe space for me. People were always nice to me, I got to hang out with the older kids on staff, and the way my dad looked at me I always knew he was proud of me. I knew how to stretch a pizza and that there was nothing more important than proper customer service before I was legally allowed to take a paycheck.

6

Committed to the
Domestication

It was now clear to me that socialization was more important than academics at school, so I found an activity that still allowed me to feel true to myself, soccer. Luckily for me, the next activity of choice after my short-lived cheerleading career was something I was much better at. I began playing soccer when I was five, and by the time I entered middle school, I was a full-blown tomboy who excelled on the soccer field. And as it appears, it was an acceptable choice of social activities, even for a girl.

Often considered to be our most awkward years, I entered into middle school feeling confident in who I was and what I was about. I could be found wearing athletic shorts, a baggie shirt, my hair in a ponytail, and the underpart of my hair buzzed nice and short. One of my earliest pet peeves was being able to feel my sweaty hair on the back of my neck when I played soccer in the Arizona heat, so I had my mom buzz it off for me!

I was one of three sixth graders to make the middle school soccer team. I was joined by two other girls who were tall, slender, model types, making me the tiniest one on the soccer field by a long shot. Regardless of my size, I had made the team fair and square just like everyone else. I felt like I had found my home!

I'm sure middle school is awkward for boys too but being an athletic girl in middle school was brutal. I vividly remember being made fun of for being flat-chested and looking like a boy when most of my other classmates were already developed and wearing makeup. However, I had learned that excelling on the soccer field was an acceptable activity for a girl, so I did my best to ignore the naysayers and focused all of my attention on the soccer field. Determined to never again be bad at anything, I committed to my good girl training and did not let anything get in my way.

7

Sticking with the Pack vs Speaking My Truth

Somewhere along the way, I found myself in the middle of a girl gang of friends, with no real recollection of how I arrived there. They were all much prettier and taller than me, some played other sports, some dated boys, but somehow, we all seemed to get along. Never in a million years would I have pegged myself as a member of this friend group.

However, the version of me that I was at home was different. It was almost as if I was living this double life. At home, I *loved* to write! I made scrapbooks and journals and was obsessed with collecting quotes on the philosophy of life and love. To this day, I still have all of my old journals and diaries full of my favorite quotes and the sagas of my early crushes.

When I sat on my bed and put pen to paper, it was like I was transformed into another dimension. It was as if I could jot down every lesson and experience from those before me and create my own perfect version of reality. I tried to share these theories with my classmates and other kids in my neighborhood, but the girls were more interested in giggling at boys and the boys were more interested in showing off for the giggling girls. It all felt so juvenile to me, for I had already experienced and gotten past my boy crazy days in elementary school.

One of my favorite pastimes, when alone in my room, was to read my favorite astronomy book. I had this one book that I would re-read over and over again, almost as if I was trying to memorize its contents. I already knew I was going to be a professional soccer player when I grew up, but my favorite career option was to be an astronomer. I knew I was smart enough to have a comet named after me one day, so I kept reading my astronomy book over and over.

One of my favorite memories with the girl gang was a giant slumber party we had on the deck of my parents' house, above the garage. We were laying out in our sleeping bags and giggling amongst the stars. In full transparency, I planned this whole idea for my birthday sleepover because I was too afraid to sleep outside all alone. I didn't care about the birthday party, I just cared about sleeping outside amongst the stars. As the girls giggled, I laid on my back and stared at the skies, dreaming of visiting the life that I knew was somewhere up there above me.

None of the other girls believed me when I shared my dreams of wanting to become an astronomer, so I just kept it to myself and let them gossip about who had just broken up and which boys were now available. After my night amongst the stars, I took my astronomy studies much more seriously. I started taking notes as I re-read my astronomy book, which quickly turned into practically just rewriting the thing cover to cover. It didn't matter to me how I absorbed the information; I just knew it was the most important book I needed to know about. I wouldn't have put it past myself to sleep with it under my pillow to absorb the information by osmosis in my sleep.

One night I woke up out of a dead sleep to see a creature sitting on the shelf of my bedroom closet. It was not a stuffed animal or anything that I had ever seen before. It was very much alive, and I was not asleep. I sat up in bed and pulled the covers up to the bottom of my eyes. Softly blinking my eyes open again, I saw the thing still sitting there. It was propped up in the closet with its knees to its chest. It had long, bumpy fingers and a spooky-looking face. It didn't have any hair, and it didn't stay long enough to speak. Watching this thing blink and look back at me, I spooked and pulled my blanket up over my eyes. By the time I was brave enough to emerge from the covers, he was gone.

Clear that my friends didn't even understand my astronomy book, I was definitely not going to try to explain the creature I had seen on the shelf in my closet. I never told a soul. Then it happened again!

I woke again from a dead sleep, in the middle of the night, in the same bedroom to find the same exact creature sitting on the shelf in my closet. As he sat with his knees tucked to his chest, I instantly knew it was him again. I caught myself gazing at him until he blinked his eyes, and I was too frightened to look any further. I tightly closed my eyes and said, "Go away, go away, go away!" I can still see him, clear as day, sitting there in my childhood bedroom, knees tucked, fingers wrapped around the shelf's edge, the other hand draped over his knees.

When I see him in my mind's eye today, he doesn't frighten me the same way because I can see so clearly that he wanted to speak to me. It was like he was waiting for me to initiate an invitation to speak, and each time that he arrived I was frightened just before he would open his mouth. It's almost like I can watch the experience from the third person, and he doesn't give the impression that he is dark or demonic. I was understandably frightened as a young girl experiencing an unknown creature in her bedroom, but looking at him today, he doesn't have the vibe that says he was there to harm me. I feel like he was just trying to speak to me.

I tried to explain him to my parents but of course, they told me it was just a dream and there was no creature in my closet. They told me I have a vivid imagination and that one day it would come in handy. From that day forward my dreams became even more vivid. Sometimes able to remember them when I awoke, I would snooze my alarm and drop back into the dream.

My dream space felt creative and safe, but the creature in my closet scared me too much, so I never slept with the closet door open again. To the best of my knowledge, he never returned to visit me. However, closing the closet door before turning off my light at night became my first obsessive-compulsive behavior, one that would take conscious unwinding well into adulthood.

After that experience, I set down my astronomy book and did my best to focus on my good girl training. At the time, that training was heavily influenced by soccer and giggling over boys. Come to find out, these boy crazy experiences are incredibly heightened after a young girl gets her first period. This happened much sooner for my girlfriends than it did for me. I was late into eighth grade before I understood what this insatiable obsession with boys was all about.

8

Seduction of the Pack

I arrived in high school with the same group of girlfriends, and the confusion of who I was began to lay on thick. I had felt comfortable and brave in yearbook class and my other creative endeavors, but the more I shared my enthusiasm for these classes, the more the eyes of my besties began to roll. Desperate to maintain my socialization, I again began to build a second life for myself. And soon, the version of who I was in the hallways was different from who I was within the safety of the yearbook studio.

While the girls I knew started dating boys in bands, I found more excuses to spend my time in yearbook. And as they started ditching lunch, I started diving into lunchtime editing. I conveniently had an editor's meeting each day they wanted to ditch lunch.

The more time I spent in the yearbook studio, the more I realized that the other kids in my class were doing the same. It was like our secret hideout, a secret party only we were invited to! As I began to distance myself from my girl gang and spend more time in the studio, another magical tidbit of fun happened. I fell in love!

He was in my grade, incredibly tall, and played volleyball. He thought I was brilliant and loved hanging out with me while I worked. We attended each other's games, were loved by each other's families, and didn't have a care in the world about pressures to lose our virginity. We were the epitome of innocent young love.

Turns out dating boys in our grade was not the cool kid thing to do, so the girls would often scoff when I chose to spend time with him instead of with the older bad boys in the bands. But we were young and in love and nothing else anyone had to say about it mattered.

One of the coolest things about being in yearbook was that we had the opportunity to attend a journalism conference for accelerated yearbook programs. My boyfriend and I were both selected to attend, and since they loved my innocent boyfriend, my parents approved for me to go. When one imagines yearbook camp, allow your brain to follow the rabbit hole of a common innuendo of band camp. That was yearbook camp!

I wasn't yet into partying or total fuckery, but I surely took advantage of the opportunities for under-the-blanket hand jobs on the back of the bus and began to explore some of the more promiscuous sides of young love. It was just enough time away from our parents to get into a little trouble, and just long enough together to realize I wanted more, more, more!

From the moment I learned about the power I had over a horny boy, it was like something completely took over me and this evil villain took over. I felt like I had complete control over this poor boy, and he suddenly transitioned from the love of my life into an object to play with. By the end of yearbook camp, I had decided that the relationship was too vanilla for me and set my eyes on some of the bad boys that hung out with the bands. The proof was within the pages of my high school diary, which I recently had the immense pleasure of thumbing through. I was crushing on the bad boys before I could even break up with my first love.

Bless his heart because I completely shattered that boy's dreams. We were going to be together forever, and I couldn't get away fast enough. I returned home from yearbook camp and dove right back into the girl gang, ready to rock and roll.

9

Choosing Social vs Self

Transitioning from the comfort zone of my yearbook years to the wild west of high school socialization was like leaving the theatre audience of a Shakespeare play and getting thrown into the middle of a mosh pit at a rock concert. It was chaotic, loud, dramatic, and ever-changing.

Committing to this socialization wasn't just a mental commitment; it was more importantly a physical one. And if I was going to try and fit in, I preferred to blend in and had no desire to be amongst the popular girls' groups. They were way too beautiful and put together than I could ever be. I could barely figure out how to blow dry my hair, let alone curl it so elegantly! That group was completely out of my league.

My girl gang was considered the second tier of the cool girls. They were pretty and social, and plenty of boys paid attention to them. And even though they weren't perfect and untouchable like the most popular girls, they were fashionable and put together enough to be the coolest girls of the obtainable groups. So I started saying yes to more sleepovers, and never missed a chance to join them on shopping trips.

From them, I learned that if I put my wet hair in a braid the night before, I could avoid the complicated blow-drying process and go straight to the flat iron in the morning. I even mastered the multicolored eyeshadow craze to shop at the popular cosmetic store. From the outside it was clear, I was one of the girls!

Just as fall rolled around, I took part in soccer tryouts and made the Varsity squad fairly young. Again, I was one of the tiniest ones on the soccer field. And just like in middle school, I was most comfortable on the pitch, and being the youngest and smallest player on the team never seemed to phase me. Except that this time, I was good enough to be taken seriously by the older girls and now pretty enough to be noticed by the soccer boys.

Even though I was building my alter ego with the girl gang, none of them ever played soccer, so that was always my special domain. The older soccer girls took me in as their 'Lil sis and I felt like I had arrived. They were nice to me in the hallway, they were much cooler than the caddy cliques developing amongst the girls in my grade. Most of my soccer friends were one or two years older than me, so I always had this escape to my other world.

Then I started getting introduced to guys on the boys' soccer team! That was another world indeed. There was something instantly seductive about a cute boy who also understood the magic of being on a soccer pitch. It was a whole demographic of boys that my girl gang had no access to. Soccer was one of the only high school sports where the girls' and boys' seasons ran at the same time. Some my age, and some older, there were always cute boys around to flirt with.

It didn't take long for me to learn that my new look and confidence from being on the varsity squad were exuding from my pours. I felt important, seen, understood, and empowered, and what other way does a high school girl have to express that energy than in the direction of cute soccer boys?

I soon learned that while I desired to blend in amongst the girl gang, I was a shining star emerging amongst the soccer community and there was this thing about me that the other girls seemed incredibly envious about. I had these big, perfect, long, luxurious full eyelashes and piercing green eyes. This was long before the age of eyelash extensions and fake lashes, and both girls and guys alike drooled over mine.

It was almost as if this secret power had been unlocked and I was the only one who had the key. I began experimenting with my eye makeup to see the variety of reactions I could get. I could wear strategically combined eyeshadow colors to make my green eyes beam out of my head. I could wear my black eyeliner just so, where the boys couldn't unlock their gaze and I could wear nothing but mascara, and the cool girls would gawk over my perfect lashes. Being invisible was no longer an option and I was learning how to play the game.

The mastery, however, came when I learned there were a variety of ways in which I could bat my eyelashes to make boys completely captivated by me. I could be running laps with my team, lock eyes with a guy, bat my eyelashes just so, and he would lose track of all space and time. None of the other girls seemed to possess this power, it was all mine.

So naturally, as any new magician or wizard would, I practiced using my new powers. I practiced and practiced and practiced until I was seductively good. The beautiful thing about being with the soccer girls compared to the cool girls in my grade was that the soccer girls weren't catty or judgmental of my new powers, in fact, they gave me an award for it!

At the End of Season Award Ceremony, as the seniors graciously accepted their well-deserved awards, I was presented with the inaugural new addition of, "Boy Crazy Queen." I was recognized among all of the graduating seniors when no one else my age was even noticed. I accepted that award as a badge of honor, and I knew my practice was paying off. My powers were growing stronger, and I began to experiment with some of the cool guys in my classes. Bad boys and soccer boys alike were intrigued and surprised by me, like I had just been seen for the very first time.

I was becoming more centralized in the circle of the girl gang, and as we moved through high school, the soccer girls in the grades above me became increasingly interested in directing their catty energy at me, especially since the guys they were chasing began to pay more attention to me. It was the first time I'd ever "stolen another girl's man", and as far as I was concerned, those girls had their chance. I took full advantage of the attention and acceptance. I was fully committed to the socialization, and my training was working.

10

When We Are Out of Alignment

High school is such a unique and beautiful time to experiment and explore who we are and what we love, that is unless we only follow what we are told to do. I dabbled in volleyball at my last school and tried out for the team in high school. To my surprise, I made the squad and was yet again the tiniest one on the team. I knew I was never going to be a professional blocker or anything that required serious hops or legitimate height, but I was a great digger and had a keen eye and the communication skills required to be a great leader.

Volleyball is all about communication on the floor, and I saw the flow and defense as plays developed. It was like I could see the court from an aerial view, like chess pieces moving about both sides of the court. It was strategic and like an elegant dance. I was truly surprised at how quickly I fell in love with this game.

As I progressed in volleyball, I continued to tremendously progress on the soccer field. I was invited to play on a traveling club team, often competing with the most elite teams in Arizona and Southern California. Between barely maintaining my status in yearbook, falling in love with volleyball, and committing to the next level of competitive club soccer, I felt like I was being pulled in every direction. With a decade of soccer experience now under my belt, my coaches and parents regularly told me that I had a real shot of playing in college.

I had known since middle school that I was going to be a professional soccer player, which was never in question. I was going to be a Tar Heel at North Carolina like my idol and pen pal, then go on to play on the U.S. National team. As my club team began hosting college prep training camps, I was told it was time to get serious. All my other "hobbies" were great and all, but it was time to choose.

Yet, while playing professional soccer had always been the plan, when the time came to choose, I couldn't help but feel a knot in my stomach. I had always felt at home in the yearbook studio, whether it was cool or not, and I fit in so naturally on the volleyball court. But could either of those things guarantee me a future?

I remember being at volleyball practice that following week with what felt like the worst acid reflux I'd ever experienced. I was on the court, deep in stance, in full flow of a drill, and just started dry heaving. My teammates looked at me like I was about to puke on them, but I kept it together long enough to keep playing.

Yearbook was easy to resolve. I had a conversation with my yearbook teacher and told her that I needed to hand off all sports photography to other staffers and that I was only able to commit to my editor duties during class and at lunch. I could still do what I needed to do during school hours for yearbook, but volleyball was a different story. It was midway through the fall season, and I had to make a choice. I had to go with the guarantee.

I decided to quit the volleyball team. I regretted it the second I walked out of the gymnasium. Certain that I had a future in soccer, I dove in 110%. I was not even a senior in high school, and I was already preparing resumes and letters of recommendation for the schools I wanted to attend. For competitive sports, we had to have these things prepared in advance because we were playing in showcase tournaments, and scouts could inquire at any moment. I harnessed my writing and editorial skills into an impressive scout package. My coaches were impressed and assured me there would be multiple offers on the table.

The showcase tournaments out of town were always steep competition. Our team was never the best, but we had many moments of brilliance and many players that were at the caliber to catch the eyes of the scouts. I knew I had to be on at all times.

At one game, in particular, I was playing left-wing and was met with another winger who was significantly bigger, stronger, faster, and taller than me. But I was there to rally, so I was not rattled. I dove deep and was able to keep up as we sparred up and down the wing together. While she was strong on offense, my time in volleyball allowed me to be low and fierce on defense. While she was fast on defense, I was strong in my footwork. I had this signature move where I would have the ball in the left-wing, juke left, pass the ball past my defender on the right, and then sprint past them on the opposite side, leaving them confused on which way to turn.

After leaving her in the dust a couple of times in the first half, she caught on to my moves. She started laying her body into me deeper and deeper, making my footwork harder and harder to break. During one play, I looked up and saw my defender beginning to cut up the middle to support me, I laid off a pass for her to take off and peel off around my opponent. She must have thought I was pulling the signature move on her again and lunged sideways to catch me as I passed.

I was just perfectly square on her left as she lunged her body directly into me. As we made contact, both of my feet left the ground and she sent me sailing past the sideline. I landed on a parent sitting in their chair. I felt the cracks throughout my body and for the slightest moment, everything around me was silent. My life flashed before my eyes, and I knew my future was at stake depending on what I did next. I closed my eyes, took a deep breath, and got out of the chair and back in the game.

The rest of the tournament, and the weeks that followed, was a blur as I found myself in and out of doctors' offices, chiropractors, and orthopedic specialists. No one could seem to find anything wrong with me, but I knew there was something very wrong.

Since no one could tell me anything was definitively wrong with my back, I kept playing. My future was at stake for god's sake!

Luckily, my parents believed me when I told them there was something wrong with my back, so my new after-school activities consisted of traction and adjustments before high school soccer practice, dinner, then club practice. I was in full-blown soccer domination and complete and utter hell at the same time. It was so incredibly painful to play, but I somehow managed to forget that anything was going on inside my body the moment I was on the pitch. Mind over matter, right?

There was something meditative for me about being under those buzzing lights, on the rock-hard Arizona ground, and amongst the faint laughter of my teammates. I often felt checked-out to everyone and everything around me, but my body knew exactly what to do as soon as it was go-time. I had been training for years!

After playing left wing most of my competitive career, I got moved to center back during my junior year. This was an unusual move for the smallest girl on the team to be the sweeper, and the final line of defense before the goalie, but I rolled with it. I instantly fell back into a familiar trance, similar to when I was on the volleyball court. I could view all the moving pieces of the chess board from above. Except my chess board was a soccer pitch, and my pieces were girls buzzing around the field. Somehow, I could see the moves being played out just before they happened in real-time, and this made me perfect for the center-back position. I could anticipate the plays coming my way and intercept them in action.

I no longer needed to be the biggest, strongest, or fastest player on the field. It was as if I got quicker, smarter, and more aggressive overnight. Always dominating with my footwork on offense, I also somehow became more confident about getting physical. If I couldn't catch you, I could perfectly time a slide tackle and stop you in your tracks. I even got my first few yellow cards that year for aggressive play. In fact, after the game where I got the very first yellow card, my mom convinced the referee to sign and date the card and let her keep it. It was humiliating and hilarious, but it was like a secret badge of honor.

Something was unleashed in me that year, and I was a completely different player. I had no fear. I took no shit, and I even developed the audacity to start shit-talking to the refs if they were not in my favor. This fire was pouring out of me, and it usually translated into really great skill.

On this one particular day, I recall my back hurting more than normal. This annoying little shit that I was playing against was just so much faster than me. I couldn't keep up with her and landed a slide tackle a bit too aggressively into her. The ref hit me with a yellow card and rage just poured out of my body towards him. It didn't take all but a moment for that yellow card to turn into a red card, landing my happy ass on the bench for the rest of the game.

Meanwhile, my back was killing me, and being on the sidelines royally sucked, so I could feel everything. In hindsight, I could have been grateful that I started and played all game, every game, because that pain coursing through my body was brutal, but the fire inside me was burning far too high for gratitude.

About halfway through my junior year, on my umpteenth visit to a specialist, someone finally found the break in my back. No one had seen it before because they were all looking on the surface of my spine. And since it wasn't a clean break, it wasn't until someone looked on the underside of the bones that they found the cracks. I had fractured the underside of my L4 and L5 vertebrae, and just like that I was no longer allowed to play.

Don't get me wrong, my schedule didn't suddenly clear up with this news. I was still the captain of both the high school and the club teams, which meant that I was still on the pitch leading my teams, I just had to do it from the sidelines while standing next to my coaches. As for my afternoon chiropractic appointments, those were now replaced with more intensive specialists and all sorts of alternative medicines.

While surgery was always on the table, I had a firm "go fuck yourself" attitude about that option. Instead, I opted for the more homeopathic option, even though I didn't for one second believe that it would work. I showed up for acupuncture and whatnot and thought it was a load of crap, so I never gave any of it the proper chance to heal me.

Soon, I was given a full torso back brace to wear, and a cocktail of herbal supplements and painkillers to take. The back brace was like a corset that started just below my breasts and had metal rods down past my hips. Getting in and out of my car was a chore, in which I less than gracefully fell in and out of the seat because I could not twist or bend in my midsection.

As the specialists added to that cocktail of supplements and painkillers, nothing seemed to work. The pain I felt after the pills wore off was the same amount of pain I felt before and after I took the pills. Nothing worked! So the doctors began moving me from the more holistic options to the gamut of pharmaceutical pain medications. It took all of about five minutes to see that the entry-level prescriptions were not going to do the trick. That's when the doctors moved me up the scale. I remember the moment, clear as day when I had my first hydrocodone.

I was laying across one of the chairs in my living room, feet dangling off the side as I popped that first pill. My body got warm, the world got a bit quieter, and my feet no longer wanted to sway. My body relaxed for the first time in eternity as I drifted off to sleep. None of the twenty-nine other pills in that bottle ever felt the same again. Convincing everyone that it still wasn't doing the trick, the doctor moved me even further up the scale and I was told that my last option would be oxycodone. I graciously accepted and went on my way.

The fire inside of me grew with each passing day until one day the most tragic news hit the field. One of our beloved boys' soccer players had died unexpectedly of meningitis that morning. We had all just watched him score the winning goal to bring home the boys' state championship two weeks prior. Our community and our teams were devastated. Ryan was a stunning, effervescent ray of sunshine, and losing him radiated through every hallway. Even surrounding schools felt the loss and sent their condolences to our teams.

Amid our immediate grief-stricken sorrows, both the girls' and boys' soccer teams were rushed to the local park where one of the fathers was handing out prescriptions for us all to immediately get the meningitis vaccine. We had all been with Ryan in his final days and were swiftly educated on how this infection spread commonly among athletes and young adults. I'll never forget the sound of his girlfriend's wails as she lay in the middle of the grass, the rest of us lined up and waiting for our prescription orders. We were all shaken to our core, and as one does when grieving a loss in high school, we solemnly planned to have a kegger in his honor.

That was one of the first times that I mixed alcohol with my new pain medications and experienced the comfort that immediately took place within my body. It was a fix I would chase down for the next decade. I had finally found something that worked! The only time I was not physically in pain or crawling in my skin was when I had just the right amount of alcohol in my system. I had to keep adding more to make sure it wouldn't wear off. Being underage, no doctor was going to give me this secret, but I had found the solution to my problems, and it was in the bottle.

11

Being Needed and Feeling
Important

Completely unable to cope, or even fathom processing through the grief of losing soccer, I did what I knew to do best, I stuffed the pain further down inside me and pretended that everything was okay. While I said goodbye to scholarships, I accepted my entrance into the local university and began coaching 13–17-year-old boys' soccer with a man I knew vaguely from the boys' program around town. Being only a year older than some of the boys didn't stop my coaching partner from bringing me on board.

He took me under his wing and taught me everything he knew. We did coach training camps and co-coached a few different boys' teams together. Being around him empowered me to stay active within the soccer community.

During the first practice I attended, he had me scrimmage with the boys. I remember every detail like it was yesterday. We were at the local park, under the buzzing lights with the older boys. Having been told that I'd never play again, I must have given him a puzzled look when he told me to get in there. "Just trust me, Morgan," he said.

I was so desperate to get back on the pitch that I trusted him. And what do you know, it was like the second my body went back into the combat zone, it remembered exactly what to do. The second

I caught a pass in the wing, it was like ecstasy raced through my body again for the first time. I looked up and knew I was home. I leaned into my defender and knew exactly what to do next. I pulled the signature move right over on him and sped by as he was still spinning in his tracks. The rest of the boys howled, and I played the ball back into the center of the pitch. Feeling over the moon to know I still had it, I looked back at my coaching partner beaming from ear to ear. "See, I told you to trust me," he said as I came back to the sideline. "You schooled them just like I knew you would and now they will take you seriously as the authority here with me."

And he was right. I went on to coach some of those boys for the next four years. It was one of the most rewarding experiences of my life watching them blossom from goofy tweens to some stand-up young men. They took me seriously, and we did work!

I'd sit and talk with my coaching partner each night after practice. Dangling my legs off the back of his truck, he would tell me about how great I was with boys and how they responded to me in a particular drill. We'd occasionally have to pull a good cop/bad cop routine, but even when I coached them alone, I always had their respect.

Just as my ego was properly greased, he would come to stand between my legs, still dangling off the bed of his truck, and kiss my forehead before I left each night, telling me how grateful he was to have me. I trusted him completely, and never thought anything the wiser. I felt so appreciated and important.

Soon he began telling me that the payments had started coming in late from the team mom and that he wasn't going to be able to pay me on time. I trusted him so I kept showing up. He started having more work things come up, so he needed me to cover more solo nights. I knew he needed me, so I kept showing up.

I'd see the team mom come up and talk to him all the time, but he would still tell me the payments were delayed. The next thing I know, months had passed without me receiving any payment, but I was so in love with coaching these boys that I kept showing up.

One day at the restaurant, while talking to my dad, I had to barricade him inside the shop because he was ready to go and punch this guy in the face for taking advantage of me. I assured him that all was well and that I would be paid. Weeks and weeks went by with no payment received. I would show up, bright-eyed and bushy-tailed, and week after week, I continued to not be paid. And every night after practice, he would kiss me on the forehead and tell me how great I did, and I would trust that the money was coming. The money never came.

One night, I was solo coaching when I saw the team mom in the parking lot and flagged her down and politely asked her when we could expect the money to arrive. She informed me that she had paid religiously on the first of every month and that my partner refused to show up if it was even one day late. She assured me that all payments were up to date, and always on time.

She must have read the confusion on my face because she then asked me, "Morgan, are you not being paid?" I shook my head, no. She scoffed and asked me for how long. When I told her how long, she was beside herself. She expressed how great of a job I was doing with the boys and how my partner was completely out of line for treating me this way. I didn't understand what was going on because he had always been so loving and affectionate with me. She promised to cut me a check directly before giving my partner his cut and would speak to him about what I was owed.

My dad was livid when he learned that his suspicions were true, and I felt strangely comforted that he wanted to punch my partner in the face for me. At the next practice, my partner handed me an envelope of cash and barely spoke to me the entire night. He scolded me in front of the boys for their goofing off, and he never touched my face in the parking lot again. He was punishing me for going behind his back to get paid. His alpha ego was bruised, and I would take the brunt of it.

Knowing that he had a temper, I took on the slack so it wouldn't be directed at the boys. When he started to get heated, I stepped in to take over the session and would invite him to go cool off. And at the end of each practice, he would collect his belongings and be out of the parking lot before some of the parents had even collected their children. I felt like I was doing the right thing by protecting the boys from his rage, but also knew that it was all my fault. I should have never said anything to the team mom. I had disrupted the magic that we had created, and it would never be the same again.

12

Numbing to Maintain
Importance

Maintaining appearances in the soccer community allowed me to remain relevant on the outside. Coaching filled my cup immensely, but I was slowly being tortured and destroyed on the inside. I began shifting into a group of friends that my family couldn't understand, as a result. I still maintained a couple of the friends I had from the high school girl gang, but the circle we rolled with was not the same. Little by little, I found myself amongst much more experienced partiers, and one particular guy took a liking to me.

I quickly learned that he was also a good kisser and that hanging around him suddenly made people act just a little bit different toward me. While I usually preferred to be invisible, being with him made me seem even cooler amongst the party kids. I started being invited to frat parties and somehow found my way into a whole other circle of college experiences that I was completely naive to. Everywhere I'd go, people seemed to think I was cool and important.

Not long after our first kiss, he became my boyfriend. I would ride in his cool car to go meet his cool mom and we would listen to cool music. It was never about staying long at his mom's, more about the drive out of town to get to her house. We would roll down the windows, blare the music, and nothing else in the world seemed to matter when he'd look over at me. One hand on the wheel, one hand in my lap, he would look at me with those glossy green eyes, and I would just melt. He was so cool!

We would arrive at his mom's house, and she would often meet us outside. She loved me and often made it a point to catch up with me. She would hand him a plastic baggie of his medications and we would be on our way. Knowing how much pain I was constantly in; he permitted me to have a few of his pills any time I needed some extra support. I was no longer getting the good stuff from my doctors since I had refused back surgery, so I needed all the help I could get.

He was the first boy through whom I learned what it meant to have wild and steamy sex. He took me to places I'd never been before with anyone else, and he taught me how deep into surrender I could go to turn pain into pleasure. I'd spend my days numbing as hard as possible with pain pills and alcohol and then when tangled up with him turn that pain into pure ecstasy. Once I had a taste of that kind of sex, I needed more, more, and more. It was not long before I'd beg him to bite me, scratch me, bruise me, anything he needed to do to get me off.

I had standards, of course. I was still living this double life as a good girl, so he wasn't allowed to touch my face and he wasn't allowed to leave hickeys on my neck. There was not much trashier than a hickey on someone's neck, and I wouldn't have any part of it. From the shoulders down, however, all was fair game. He would make me bleed, leave bite marks on my skin, and bruises of every shape and color. I carried them as badges of honor of the wild sex life we had, with no regard to anyone else's thoughts or opinions.

We would often have people over at my house and I hated it so much because I knew we were way too loud and too disruptive on weeknights, but people still loved to come over, so I rolled with it. It was common for a few people to pop in and out regularly, but on the nights that turned into full-blown parties, I couldn't drink enough to stop my skin from trying to crawl off my bones, so I would retreat into my bathroom and pull out the bottle that I kept tucked under the sink. I would pull out a few of the pills from my boyfriend's baggie and chase them down with a couple of swigs of the under-the-sink vodka.

Then I would sit fully clothed on the toilet while I waited for them to kick in. The second my mind would get quiet enough to not think much, I would find my way back to the party. Everyone would be so wasted no one even noticed how long I'd been gone. This became the normal routine, and no one seemed to be the wiser.

13 |

Creative Genius

Toward the end of my freshman year of college, I got sick. I was incredibly depressed, insanely anxious, and had been diagnosed with the West Nile virus. My next-door neighbor had a mosquito-infested koi pond, so I accepted the diagnosis as truth and went about my studies at the University.

On the days when I had Astronomy, I always found a way to be on time and clear-headed, but on the days when I had Russian History, I would have an alarm set to leave the party house to get to class. Most mornings I was still drunk and in the previous night's clothes. As my first semester was approaching its end, I was often violently ill by mid-morning. I would be in the bathroom dry heaving, and by the time I made it home from class, I would just sit and shake on the bathroom floor. My doctors prescribed me a slew of anti-anxiety and antidepressants, but nothing had a chance of working because I would just throw it all up. The only thing that calmed my nerves was a cigarette, a drink, or a couple of my boyfriend's pills. But no matter what combination I tried, I only got worse. I ended up getting so ill that I missed most of my finals and was placed on academic probation on account of failing most of my first semester classes.

So sick and tired of being sick and tired, I struggled to find any motivation to continue with my four-year degree in human psychology. It was around this time that I saw an ad for a photography program at a local art college and immediately applied. Art school sounded way more fun, and at that moment I was no longer willing to commit to eight more years of college to enter into the psychology field. Halfway through my second semester at the university, I was accepted into the photography program, beginning first thing in the summer. With none of my credits transferring except for one of my Spanish classes, I gave myself the green light to live it up for the next couple of months until it was time to get serious. After all, I deserved a break. I had been in school for over 13 years, every year, just like a good girl was supposed to be.

I instantly fell in love with art school. It was a significantly smaller campus, and most of the people were quite weird. With my background in yearbook and film photography, I was already a few steps ahead in my introductory classes. I immediately stepped into my self-proclaimed role as teacher's pet, and I knew I had arrived!

There was something sexy about art school. Everyone was so creative and brilliant, and it wasn't the same party scene as at the university. It was normal to lounge about campus smoking cigarettes, and lunches at the bar on the corner were the norm for all levels of students. There weren't cool kid groups or popular cliques. There were just a variety of creatures from every department. There were the well-put-together girls in the interior design program. There were the dorky but cool guys in animation and illustrations. Then the elaborately moody geniuses of the fine arts program. We had our own building for Photography and Fine Arts, and it was like our own little hideout of creative fuckery.

I was enamored by the older fine arts students, and so desperately wanted what they had. I became obsessed with art history and thrived in my creative writing classes. Being in art school was like being whisked away to post-war New York City where all the creatives had migrated from Europe and were collectively and individually rewriting the notion of what art could be. We were allowed to be messy, loud, bold, and moody, and that was my jam!

I carried this energy I was channeling in the brilliance and insanity of early 20th century artists, so my drinking, smoking, and fucking away my feelings were all part of the experience. I had found my people, and my behaviors were all cosigned by the artist archetype I so longed to be a part of.

Unlike my time at the university, I showed up every day, and I had a new sense of purpose that fueled my ego and importance. I received slightly above-average grades, but that's the beautiful thing about creating art, its importance is all a matter of perception. I excelled in the areas that I cared about and was perfectly mediocre in the areas that I didn't. For me, art school was all about sticking it to the man and breaking this notion that I had to get a corporate job, get married, have two point five kids, and have my life settled by the time I was twenty-five. No, thank you! I was not about that life.

I graduated with my four-year degree in three years and gave them a big fat "hell no!" when they asked me to purchase my cap and gown and participate in their graduation ceremonies. I was giving my Artist Talk and had a BFA Thesis Exhibition with my homegirl, so I didn't need any other fluff and bullshit to commemorate my accomplishments. There were only two of us graduating from our program that semester, so we shared this big, beautiful gallery space just the two of us!

My senior thesis was all about my experience living through a deployment with my military boyfriend. We had met at a party, and I instantly knew there was something special about him. He said all the right things and was so impressed with my bravery for following my dreams as an artist. He was a musician but always resented having to put on his monkey suit and show up for the man every day. I was his muse, and we fell head over heels in love.

Dating him opened me up to a whole other world of parties. I learned very quickly that I was not like the other military girlfriends and that I was much more comfortable drinking with the big boys. The melding of my military friends and my art school friends was a natural blend. They all had strength for partying and playing pool. My overly competitive side was right at home with the boys, and it wasn't long before many of his friends began taking notice of me.

I was faithful to my core, but you better believe that I loved the attention and the way those boys made me feel important. I had bodyguards everywhere I went, and could party as hard as I wanted to, knowing someone always had my back.

When it came time for my boyfriend to be deployed, I already knew I had a built-in support system amongst his buddies, even when I couldn't stand their girlfriends. I made the decision long ago that I was the cool girlfriend and carried myself like the seasoned deployment wives. I kept my composure. I never let anyone know how much I missed him, and I buried myself in my schoolwork.

That senior thesis was the hardest and most rewarding thing I had ever done. My professors challenged me every single day and I had no choice but to blast through my fear of standing up in confrontation when constantly being berated with insistent questions of "Why?" "Why!" Why???" I was forced to take a stand and be able to defend myself to earn the wall space in that gallery.

Everything else seemed so superficial, so I created about the one thing I couldn't share with anyone else. I created art about what it was like being on the home front of a deployment. To this day I can feel the pain in my body from that second to last semester, being in tears every single day trying to figure out how to speak about the intensity of my work. I was so hell-bent on it being successful that I showed up each day, dug deeper and deeper to attempt to answer my professor's proverbial "why." In hindsight, it was probably the exact therapy I needed to survive that experience. I would give everything I had to my thesis committee classes and then drink my sorrows away behind the mask of competitive creative genius.

Delivering that artist talk and being interviewed by the local news in a military town was one of the highlights of my life. The only thing that could have made that moment more perfect was if he had been there. And then, suddenly, he arrived, and I was the center of attention and had the man of my dreams there looking back at me. Mission accomplished.

Self-Reflection Opportunity

- Have you ever met someone and immediately felt like you have known each other for a lifetime? List those relationships and the roles they each play in your life currently. How have those relationships evolved, changed, or been removed from your life?
- Now knowing that we each have both masculine and feminine energies within us, which do you feel you lead with?
- As a young child, did you experience more positive rewards or painful punishment in your household?
- Explain how this common reward/punishment trend varied or stayed relatively the same for you in grade school.
- How did you relate to other kids your age?
- How did you feel different than other kids your age?
- Whose love did you crave the most as a child, your mother or your father?
- What did you have to do to receive their love?
- Who did you have to be to receive their love?
- What passions did you not pursue because you believed it wasn't cool?
- Have you ever pursued any passions you once were too afraid to out of fear of not being accepted? What were they? How did it feel to pursue them anyway?
- How does it feel for you to hide your authentic self?
- When you were in high school, did you choose to be the ideal of acceptance or start rebelling? Explain.

- Make a list of things you have done to avoid deep inner work. (i.e. shopping, eating, drinking, self-sabotage)
- In what ways have you rebelled against society?
- Make a list of relationships where you feel you've been taken advantage of. Explain what each experience meant to you and the current status of that relationship. (Is it still active, did you stand up for yourself, have they been removed from your life)

2

The Crumbling

14

Drop Everything + Come to His Rescue

The art school I attended was known for offering subpar aid to its students. In my self-seeking ways, I decided that this was not acceptable and that if I was going to go into that much debt to obtain this degree, then I was going to be supported in the ways that I needed to be supported. So I landed myself a job within the administrative offices at the school. I started as a receptionist and quickly worked my way into the Student Services office, where I could make a difference - a.k.a. get what I needed.

I worked in the office for two years before graduating and did successfully get all of my needs met. I cannot say that that was the experience for many other students who found their way through this institution. However, once I had weaseled my way into the good graces of the financial department, I became an ally for as many students as I could. Students began to contact me directly to inquire about their financial aid. I would walk my happy little ass over to the Financial Aid office and ask my questions. When the task in question was not handled as the student needed, I would just take it upon myself to hang out until it was processed.

I told myself that as long as I was getting my needs met then I may as well see who else I could help while I was there! Coworkers used to express in complete disbelief, "I can't believe you just waltz right in there," when I would walk into the Dean's or other executive's offices. To which I would respond, "How else are you supposed to get anything done just waiting around for them to respond to you?!" In hindsight I probably didn't have the best boundaries for protocol and procedures, but hey! No one told me to stop. So I didn't.

This experience significantly spearheaded my career in higher education. Now before you go get your panties in a bunch thinking, "Wait, Morgan - didn't you go on to use your degree that you worked so hard to achieve?" Deep breaths. Yes, I did. While still in Tucson, I began working for a very prestigious photography studio in town. The grounds were stunning, the studio was gorgeous, I had every tool and toy available at my disposal, but there was a problem. The renowned photographer who created this gem had passed away and it was all now being run solely by his widow. My high school graduating class was the last year to have senior portraits done directly by him before he passed. He was a very special man.

Knowing that his name carried much clout around town, I knew that I would work there anyway and allow his legacy to propel my photography career. I worked at the studio with his widow and another photographer, soaking up every ounce of experience that I could. Banking on the clout of his name around town, we were often invited to be the official photographers for high-end philanthropic events. We attended the schmanciest galas and rubbed elbows with all sorts of notable members of society. All very impressive if you are into that sort of thing.

Shortly after I graduated, my boyfriend also completed his term of duty in the military and was ready to attend the trade school of his dreams. As a perfectly doting girlfriend, desperate to get out of my hometown, I packed my bags and we headed up north to the big city. Arriving in Phoenix, a hundred miles out of my hometown, I found myself a job working at a photography studio in a department store.

Holy moly was that an experience! I quickly learned that I had more knowledge and experience than everyone else that I worked with and immediately set off to find ways to restructure how this place operated. To my surprise, one does not just waltz into a big box corporation and demand the conditions and procedures be augmented to meet one's needs. This should have been my first red flag that this would become a toxic environment for me. However, I had gotten my way many times before, so I would not surrender that easily.

Here's the thing about creative endeavors, being told what to do and how to do it doesn't often fare well for the artist. Coming off my high-end experience in Tucson, I couldn't understand how people arriving for these services could be so awful. In those moments, I had no regard for the fact that the clientele that shopped at this particular store was the same clientele showing up in my studio. I was in a very different world here, and I did not enjoy it one bit!

Determined to support my man, I forced myself to see it through. I would call my mom on my commute home every day to tell her about the wretched clients I had to entertain that day. These were full-on vent sessions, dripping with disdain. My gracious mother would just listen and console me every single day, day after day. She would remind me that this experience would open the door to the next thing and that this was all temporary. Soon, I was calling her on my commute to work as well.

I would be so anxious before even leaving the house that I would be sweating by the time I got into my car. It felt like the intensity grew deeper and stronger within my chest throughout the drive. I felt like I could just burst into tears at any given moment. I didn't know what else to do, so I would call my mom. Mile after mile, she would do her best to listen to me vent. Still doing my best to arrive safely, I would drive down the highway just bawling my eyes out. By the time I arrived at the studio, she would have to talk me off the ledge just so I could calm down enough to clean up the mascara streaming down my face. This should have been another red flag, but continuing to paint red flags green, I continued working at the studio for a few more months.

I was so desperate to support my boyfriend because I felt that he had supported me through my senior thesis. And every day that I worked at the studio, I would completely bury my true feelings from him by the time I got home. I would sit in my parked car, staring at myself in the mirror, having to give myself a pep talk just to go inside. I would project any inquiry of my day back to him and his studies, making us dinner, keeping up the house, and desperately drinking to subside the nauseating aching inside my body.

After an embarrassing explosion at my studio supervisor one day, I had to excuse myself and pace up and down the Tupperware aisle of the department store just to keep from crying. But with every turn of my heel, my blood would boil even more intensely. I didn't see any way out, and the fluorescent lights felt like they were closing in on me. I knew what I had to do.

I marched myself back over to the photo studio, where my supervisor still looked stunned that I had even walked away. I walked right past her at the checkout counter and tinkered around cleaning up the studio until the remaining customers were gone. The second I heard their goodbyes, I waltzed right up to my supervisor and unloaded all of my thoughts before she could even ask me if I was okay. I told her that I thought the procedures and bureaucracy at the company were a load of horseshit. I told her that I was incredibly miserable and that this job had ruined photography for me forever. I told her that I was going to finish out my schedule and then find a new job somewhere else because I couldn't bear one more moment in this minimum wage hellhole!

She, quite gracefully, received my rant. "I'm really sorry to hear that you feel that way," she said, "None of your points are wrong, this place really sucks. But I was also going to talk to you about becoming a manager so I could train you to replace me."

Completely not surprised that this would be the response to convince me to stay, I said, "You're smart for getting out. There aren't enough zeros to make me take your job. Sorry!"

And just then my next session arrived, and I instantly turned my freak-out rage off and my bubbly ray-of-sunshine personality back on. That was the last time I ever returned to that studio. My supervisor covered the rest of my shifts and told me I didn't have to finish out my two weeks.

After some time of alcohol-induced fuzziness, I finally found myself back in higher education. It was not at a university but at one of those trade schools that you hear about on TV. You know, the ones that promise you a better life, transferable credits, and a solution to all your problems, but never actually deliver? So desperate to never go back to a soul-sucking photography studio, I was able to get my foot in the door of the admissions department for an entry-level opening. I didn't even care what the job was, as long as it wasn't a photography studio.

As I do with all things, I dove headfirst into my new job. First on my mind was to establish myself as a high-performing leader on my team. Next was to befriend all of the cutest and coolest members of the team to establish new drinking buddies. Third was to insert my foot into every possible opportunity that was available for me to climb the corporate ladder, even some that on paper weren't even available to me. It's funny how much self-seeking and ambition resemble each other.

Within the organization, I completed leadership training certifications, leader as a coach certification, overcoming obstacles, and negotiation certifications, you name it, I completed it and excelled! I became so deeply involved within the company advancement programs that they started inviting me to help develop and assist in future training programs.

Over the next three years, I was promoted multiple times, scaled across departments, and found myself in a very prestigious position within Student Services - specializing in student retention. The secret to my success: I had such a disdain for the beast that was this type of business that I made it my mission to make damn sure that by the time a student got to me in Student Services, after already signing their life away to Admissions, I would get them to graduation!

I excelled in this position because I was able to connect with my students in a way that most other advisors didn't seem to do. I got to know them. I listened to their stories, and I dug for the truth about why they were there. Why had they made the deal with the devil in order to better their lives? My students opened up to me and they trusted me.

I was often asked by the higher-ups within the company, why my phone calls with my students were so much longer than those of most of the departments. I explained that I wasn't going to hang up the phone until we had solved the problem at hand, or my student had come off the ledge while previously ready to give up on their dreams. Simply put, I was committed to my students, and I wasn't willing to hang up the phone with them just to meet the corporate metrics. Providing my students with a true ally and support system, when most of them had nothing and no one, was my way of sticking it to the man. It was my way of rebelling against the corporate requirements, dictated by stockholders, who only viewed these brave humans as a number on their analytics. It was disgusting to me, and I stuck by my students to my core.

In hindsight, what I was doing was making the institution a lot more money in financial support by increasing the graduation rate of the school. Either way, my students always came before corporate bureaucracy. And to this day, that is a core value of mine that has not changed. I will always show up to support my people, no matter the hot water they may find themselves in. I poured my heart and soul into this work, giving to it far more than my salary provided in return. It filled my cup, while I had no idea that my world was falling apart.

On what started as a normal day in March 2013, I received a phone call from my mother. I was unable to understand her with the surrounding noise coming from the call center floor, so I walked outside to take her call. This time, my mom was the one bawling. Through her sobs, she explained to me that my dad was in the hospital, and I needed to get back home immediately.

I went back into the office, grabbed my supervisor, and headed into the HR office without a word. I sat them down and told them that I needed both of them to authorize my paperwork for an FMLA leave and that I needed to go at once. And they did.

I was granted a thirty-day paid leave of absence, grabbed my belongings, and walked out of the building knowing deep in my core that I would not be returning. My roommates couldn't understand what was happening when they returned home to find me packing. As it would turn out I wouldn't return there either, it damn near broke my best friendship. She felt completely and unexpectedly abandoned, and I could not even explain my decisions. Everything was changing before I could even comprehend what was happening. I got in my car and drove to Tucson.

My dad was the strongest person I knew. He was healthy, worked hard, rode his bicycle thirty to forty miles a day, he was a perfect bill of health. Arriving in Tucson, I learned that my dad had just had a heart attack. My brain could not comprehend how this could happen. He was a perfect bill of health! With my dad now being operated on, having a stent put in his heart, and my mom a mess, I immediately went into my role of the household: Lock it up and hold it all together. I sent my mother and brother home to get some rest and stayed the night with my dad in the hospital. With no concern about my physical state, I slept by the foot of his bed in a hospital chair. Finally feeling assured that he was in the best care, I was finally able to drift off to sleep.

In the middle of the night, I was jolted awake by the sound of sirens and alarms. The monitors connected to my dad were going bananas. His vitals were dropping. I sat helplessly as the single nurse on the floor came running in and immediately went for the incision in his groin and started what looked like CPR to his leg. A constant pitch I can never un-hear was ringing in the air - my dad was flatlining right before my very eyes. The nurse put every ounce of their weight into my dad's leg. They damn near beat the blood clot into dissolving as I sat helplessly in my chair, holding my breath. After watching his body turn completely colorless, the machines began to chirp again. I exhaled in relief.

As vitals slowly began to display on the machines again, the nurse stepped back from my dad. He was ghost white; a sight I have yet to unsee. This womxn single-handedly saved my dad's life, right before my eyes. I wept silently. Still trying to catch my breath, I knew deep within my core I was not returning to my old life. I was needed here. My dad would not go back to work for over a year, and it was my responsibility to keep the family restaurant afloat. I dropped everything I was doing and stepped into my new duties.

My good girl training taught me this was the right thing to do. Abandon everything you thought was best for you and be of service to your family when they needed you. Period. Hard stop.

I was needed. I was important. I created the much-needed stability. I was the glue. So I stayed.

15

Breaking My One Rule

Stepping into this new role as a family savior was both addictive and incredibly dysfunctional. At the ripe age of twenty-four, this was one of the hardest years of my life. Having worked in the restaurant most of my life, picking up these responsibilities was no big deal. I immediately went in and got everything organized to my standards, evaluated the staff, and all areas of opportunity for progressive change.

This primarily meant revamping my dad's filing system of "pin anything important to the wall." Being a fine art student who was prepared to get a graduate degree in curatorial studies, my eyeballs would twitch every time I stepped into the office and saw the millions of push pinholes in the walls. I took every piece of dusty paper off the walls, spackled in all the pinholes, and painted the office green. Like green, green.

It didn't take long for my entire life to be consumed by only a few tasks: Wake up, open the shop, work all day, close the shop, go to the gym, stop for a carne asada burrito and bottle of wine, and go home to shower and sleep. I was really grateful to be training at a small, local gym that was open twenty-four hours a day, and more often than not I was the only one in the weight room in the middle of the night. I loved it! I could blast my favorite metal into my headphones and rock the fuck out.

Nothing was more satisfying to me than a heavy leg day. I was a freaking beast, and progressively increasing my PRs week after week. Weight training this way made me feel alive. It made me feel significant. It made me feel a sense of control. I was constantly striving for more and it was no surprise that weight training became my new addiction. A healthy addiction!

That may be true for some people, but I do things one of two ways - all in or all out. There is no healthy middle ground for me. I go balls to the wall, or not at all. The truth of the matter is that this weight training addiction was a convenient distraction from everything else that was going on in my life. That bottle of wine I would pick up with my post-gym burrito was actually multiple bottles of wine. Every night. Each, and every, day.

I understood from a very young age that alcoholism runs in my family. This was the sole reason why I never let myself experiment with hard drugs; I knew I would like it. I'd always been told that I have a very addictive personality, but I had a code.

A code of ethics, a pact I made with myself early on in high school was that I would never do hard drugs. I was totally fine with experimenting with pot and taking my pain pills, but anything more was a hard no for me. There was also one person I knew who, in my view, was the epitome of an alcoholic and she was a hot mess all of the time. Part two of my code was that if I was never as bad as her, I would be okay. That was my standard of living and perception of right and wrong. Period.

But that's the funny thing about alcoholism, it has an interesting way of developing the fine-tuned skill of self-justification which allows us to convince ourselves about just about anything. Unbeknownst to me at the time that allowed for a lot of grey areas within my black and white code of ethics.

This cycle of wake, work, weight train, drink, and sleep progressed as the months went on. I got in the best shape of my life, and I was feeling sexy AF. I decided it was the perfect time to start online dating. However, I wasn't going to sign up for just any ol' trashy swipe right hookup app, I was going for the more sophisticated online dating sites. I signed up and was immediately flooded with conversation requests and super-hot suiters. I made it very clear that I was not looking for a relationship, as I was much too busy for that. I was looking for a committed friends-with-benefits situation, and I was not interested if you were seeing other people. In hindsight, that sounds an awful lot like a monogamous relationship to me. Using my words has always been a gift of mine, so it was easy for me to know exactly what to say and get exactly what I wanted. Online dating was great!

While the sex was great for stress management, the deeper I went into this cycle, the more I was needing more wine to be able to go to sleep at night. I would finish a bottle and would need just one more glass to calm my mind down enough for bed. Just as quickly as the second bottle would be opened, I would look up and it would be gone. A two to three-bottle night became the norm in order for me to sleep.

After every night of drinking alone in my apartment, I would wake up and hop in the shower. Like clockwork, as the water would be washing off my face, I would start to get a feeling of acid reflux in my chest. I would take a deep breath and then immediately start excessively gagging and dry heaving. This had been such a normal experience since college that I didn't think anything of it. I'd get myself together enough to open the restaurant and get to work, all the same, no one would be the wiser. I didn't like to go out to bars because I felt that I had too many skeletons in my hometown that I wasn't willing to face. So, I stuck to my little routine of work, gym, wine. Work, gym, wine.

This is where shit got real. With my code of ethics still intact, I was about five months into this new routine of running the shop, feelin' sexy, drinking all the wine in private, and feeling on top of the world. I had everything under control.

Then one day, late in the summer, I attended a function with my parents at a high-end resort in town. We had dinner plans and a social gathering by the fires in the evening, but the day was ours to lounge by the pools and relax. With my oversized hat and black sunglasses, I flagged down the bartender and ordered a margarita. It was a perfect margarita, delivered by a hot guy with a great smile, even garnished with a paper umbrella. I could finally take a load off and relax. I pulled out my phone, perfectly situated my sexy legs, and snapped a picture of my poolside umbrella drink. After I posted it online, I ordered mom and me a round of shots to get the pool party started! There is not much better than the instant burn and sigh of relief produced by a good shot of tequila and lime. It was a perfectly relaxing day in the Arizona sunshine!

I can recall on one hand the number of times I remember blacking out in my drinking career. I can particularly recall three times when I blacked out intoxicated, and it's like I watched it happen. I remember the exact moments before the blackout, the "going into the blackout," and coming out of the blackout. I was just not ever a serial blackout artist like some drinkers. That day at the pool at the fancy resort was one of those days.

After a perfect day, consisting of plenty of margaritas, it was time to collect our things and get ready for dinner. The dinner was boring and swift, as everyone was more excited for the cocktail party that was to follow. Making our way back outside to the patio overlooking the city, I stopped by the bar to discover the chili-infused tequila the resort was specializing in. There was not much more I loved in this world than a good chili-infused tequila! I could recall there only being one other place that made an infused tequila as good as this one, and that was back in Santa Monica. I was in heaven. What a perfectly relaxing and enjoyable day!

I sat alone at the bar for a moment while everyone else got settled out on the terrace. The city views were spectacular. I love the summer nights in Arizona as the cotton candy skies transition into desert city lights. Double tequila in hand, I ordered another before I could make my way to the group. I took a big swig and mustered up the moxie to join the party. With both glasses in hand, I found my way to an empty seat around the fire. I was so content by this perfect tequila-infused day that I got lost in the flickers of the flames.

Then one of the glasses almost slipped out of my hand, and my awareness was jolted from the fire. I regained my composure and settled back into my seat, my gaze caught by Lady Drinks-A-Lot, the one person I have deemed to be the epitome of an alcoholic. She was belligerent and overly obnoxious, and I couldn't stand to even look at her.

I reverted my attention to my tequilas and gazed back into the fire. As I did so, I had this deep knowing from the pits of my soul that I was about to blackout. Everything else around me grew quiet and I felt completely at peace. As I was entering the blackout, I heard one faint message spoken from within my body, "You are on her level." And then poof, I blacked out.

My parents and I were sharing a hotel room that night, and as I came to in the morning, they were both already awake. Fully clothed and sitting on the bed next to me, they peered over their coffee cups as if waiting for me to wake up. Before I could even pull my feet out of bed, they began sharing all of the completely embarrassing and mildly illegal shenanigans I had gotten myself into the night before.

As they went on, I remembered nothing. They told me all about my after-hours activities; breaking into the pool and coercing poor behavior upon a few younger minds that were present for the evening. I still remembered nothing. Looking from my mom, who was doing most of the talking, my dad gave me a look I have only ever seen one other time in my life. The look that said, "I'm not mad, I'm just disappointed." My heart shattered. I had completely failed my good girl training.

I racked my brain trying to remember, and there was nothing. There was absolutely nothing after that moment, gazing across the fire, two double tequilas in my hands, and those five painful words repeating back to me. "You are on her level." I was mortified.

Now having but a few minutes to get ready and get out of there, I threw on my work clothes, kissed my parents goodbye, and bolted as quickly as I could from that hotel room. Out of breath by the time I got in my car to head to work, something somber had happened. Before leaving the parking structure of the high-end resort, I had downloaded a sobriety tracker app on my phone. There was no thought about it. There was no conversation within myself. There was only what I can call divinely led action that took control of my fingertips in those moments.

I had betrayed my code of ethics. The pact was broken.

That moment, alone in my car, leaving the resort, I saved the time and date in the tracker, and it began to tick.

16

Now That My Good Girl
Training Had Failed

I don't do anything lightly. I am not the type of person that can say, "Oh! I will do this thing for seven days, or thirty days, or whatever number of days." I will come up with a million, completely justified, reasons to not complete said challenge. I am an all-in or all-out type of gal. So as the days grew between me and that sobriety tracker, I began to twitch. I knew in my gut that I would never be able to do something like this if I told myself, "Oh, I'll just stop drinking for thirty days," as tons of people do at various points of the year in normal society. I knew with absolute certainty that this had to be a lifestyle change or it would never work for me. It was that same knowing inside of me that told me I had broken the code I had with myself.

Incredibly confused, embarrassed, and uncomfortable, I decided that this was a totally logical step in my fitness journey. It was no secret to anyone that I was dedicated to getting my sexy on and addicted to my weight training practice. Having plateaued a little, I decided that cutting alcohol was the next logical step.

As I had been very public on social media about the successes of my fitness journey, I began to share about cutting alcohol out of my diet as the next phase of my commitment. I began receiving shock and kudos from all sides of the internet and my personal life. I continued with my simple life in Tucson: open the restaurant, work all day, close up, and head to the gym. Except that now, I had to find the willpower to drive straight home, instead of to the store for my bottles of wine.

Every night after the gym I would sit in my car, unable to turn over the ignition. I would sit there in the dark, under the one parking lot light, and pull out my phone. I would share on social media how kickass my workout was, alongside my sweaty selfie, and then muster up the courage to convince myself this not drinking thing was a good idea. It was almost as if posting about it on the internet made it real enough so that I had to maintain the image. As the vanity metrics began to roll in, validating the post I had just made, I would gather the courage to drive home. Even while the internet and the smokin' hot guys I was seeing completely validated my physical appearance, I couldn't help but notice a deeply rooted feeling of shame and disappointment within myself. So I would turn on my car, roll down the windows, crank up the jams, and tell myself, "Tomorrow I will set another PR in the gym!"

I carried on this way every day, constantly ignoring the embarrassment and shame I felt inside, while continuously throwing myself into work and the gym. The physical results were obvious, so it was easy to justify my new lifestyle. By the grace of something holy that I didn't understand, I happened to open my sobriety tracker one day to see that it had been exactly thirty days since my last drink. It was the self-justification that poured into my mind at that moment, saying I had earned a celebratory case of wine, which made something crystal-fucking-clear. I had a drinking problem. It had taken every single one of those thirty days of lying to myself, and others, before I could see myself clearly. I was an alcoholic. At that moment I knew that was the god-honest truth, and I told no one.

One Saturday night some of my mom's friends came into the restaurant for dinner. They were dressed to the nines in their western gear. Fully equipped with their bedazzled belts and fancy boots, they came in for the pregame before heading to the country bar next door. I knew that Saturday nights were poppin' over there because our parking lot would be full the second our dinner rush was over. I was no stranger to serving a slice and a beer to a dapper man in a cowboy hat, but I had never gone dancing there.

My mom's friends were professionally trained dancers, in all forms, and somehow convinced me to join them after work and said that they would teach me how to country dance. Willing to try anything that would keep me from sitting alone in my apartment at night, I agreed. I prayed those few drunken lessons in the living room with my bestie in Phoenix would come back to me. I got off work that night, threw on some jeans and my fake boots, and headed over to the bar.

Holy moly! From the moment I stepped onto that dance floor I - FELL - IN - LOVE.

Country dancing is sexy, high-energy, and exhilarating! Plus, have you seen a fine-ass cowboy who can dance?! I mean come on! What's a girl to do? The only thing sexier than a cowboy who can dance is Channing Tatum in those sweatpants grinding on his workbench, but it would still be a few years before I would meet my Channing Tatum look-alike boyfriend. This bar was country heaven and mama was hooked! Mmm ... mmm - I love me a man who can dance!

Joining this Saturday night dance crew quickly became a regularly scheduled activity for me. I was on a first-name basis with the owner, a regular to all the bouncers, and had no time to worry about not drinking while I was dancing my heart out into the wee hours of the morning. I would go home completely exhausted and on cloud nine. Life was good!

It didn't take long before the old men that I loved to dance with, the burly bouncer, and my regular Saturday night dance parties quickly became nice distractions from all those feelings still trying to bubble up inside of me. I was fit, active, hot, and socializing without alcohol - my mental health was fine! Until it wasn't.

While my extracurricular activities kept me plenty distracted after hours, things at the restaurant were getting rocky. It had now been months since my dad's episode, and while he desperately wanted to return to working in the restaurant, it was obvious to me that he was not okay. He would come into the shop and just mosey around. He would open the freezer, tinker on the computers, but wouldn't do anything. He just wanted to be around. I wanted him to be around, but he just started doing weird stuff.

He would go stand in the walk-in, and just look around. He would walk away any time the phone rang instead of answering it, and refused to make eye contact when customers wanted to see how he was doing. Folks would get so excited to see he was there, shout his name, and he would turn on his heels and walk out the back door.

He seemed to be in such a dark funk from the heart attack. Feeling like he had no purpose, being an alpha male watching his twenty-something-year-old daughter save and run his business, he was not his normal self. He was grouchy, bitter, and kind of mean. He was not the man I knew and loved, my best friend, or my ride or die. I don't know who that person was. He was lost and broken, and it broke my heart into a million pieces.

Then he started coming in and barking orders at the staff, many of whom had been hired by me and had never worked with him. He would scream at them to do something that was the polar opposite of the procedures I had been operating with for months. The staff would be confused and not know who to listen to or if what they were doing was right. I would assure them that he would be going home soon and ask them to get back to their work.

That would just kindle his fire, and he would turn his attention toward me. It was like he had developed a new hobby of trying to pick fights with me. My dad and I had never so much as argued, yet now we were constantly fighting. It broke my heart to hear the berating things he said to me, but I knew I had to maintain composure in front of my team. In the middle of his tirade, I would walk him out the back door, so the attention was all on me, and not on the staff. Then he would storm off to his car after not getting a reaction out of me, and peel out of his parking spot. Watching him leave, I would crumble to the ground.

I was heartbroken and our relationship was in shambles. I could not believe how hard he was taking this cardiac recovery. As the fights grew more frequent, and my heart continued to shatter, he was also starting to make the team uncomfortable. I eventually had to ban him from coming into the restaurant. This was the longest he had ever been out of work, but my role was to keep the ship afloat, so I did what I felt I had to do.

It almost broke us. My desperation to repair my good girl training told me that no matter what I felt, it was my responsibility to lock it up and keep the family business alive. No matter the cost. No matter the consequence. I would not let it fail. I would not fail - again.

Eventually, as the desert fall gained a crisp chill in the air, some folks who love me sat me down for what appeared to be a come-to-Jesus moment. They lovingly expressed their concerns over my well-being and mental health. My mental health! I haven't had a drink in months, I thought, didn't they know I was invincible!

I put on my good girl mask and carried on. I refused to give in or show any weakness. But deep inside, their words shattered my heart even more. They were right.

Every week that passed, I grew more uncomfortable, and with each passing week, I poured myself deeper into the restaurant. More gym sessions were being replaced with nights out dancing at the country bar, and my after-hour bliss was now being filled with hallow sex with a man I knew I'd never keep.

Those simple weeks turned into repetitively numb months until one day, in early spring, I had another deep knowing. This time it told me that as long as I stayed in Tucson, my dad would never be able to make it back to the restaurant. I knew this was a rip-off the Band-Aid type of situation. I had to completely remove myself and force his hand, or he would never get better. He would either sink or swim, and that thought was fucking brutal.

This went against everything my good girl training had taught me. However, I felt like I was slowly dying inside and had to give it a chance, plus I still hadn't told anyone how challenging things had gotten for me.

On the day I called my dad and gave him my one week's notice, I told him Friday would be my last day working at the restaurant and that I would be gone by midweek the following week. I hung up the phone before he could even respond. Then, melting past the edge of my couch onto my living room floor, I cried for the first time in over a year. And I made it count.

That following Wednesday, I moved to Los Angeles. I drove away knowing that at any moment it could all go up in flames, but I couldn't carry that responsibility any longer. I had to get out of there. Driving out of town that day was one of the hardest things I'd ever done.

Arriving in Santa Monica, I bunked up at my aunt and uncle's house and found a job almost instantly. I was hired as the director of marketing for a private personal training company. The owner had outgrown his ability to grow the business himself, and my business savviness was just what he needed to organize and scale his business. I found myself able to train for free in gorgeous westside gyms, and the clients began rolling in. It was all working out!

It was all working so well that the owner of the company started spending more time away. Frequenting Las Vegas, partying, and participating in quite lavish dates in Malibu. This was proof that I was doing a great job! My good girl training had been reinstated. That was until my paychecks started bouncing.

He was spending the money faster than I could bring it in. Without a paycheck in LA for seven weeks I was beyond desperate! Anyone who has ever lived in Los Angeles can attest to the fact that it is not cheap. Unwilling to see his faults, I couldn't fight him any longer. I had to find another job and going back to Tucson was not an option.

On a Sunday evening, while sitting on my bed, I came across the most generic job posting on the internet. It read something along the lines of, *Receptionist Needed! Must be able to start immediately!* SOLD.

Desperate to make it work in LA, I applied for the job and received a note back that very same night and had an interview set for the following morning.

17

Beyond Desperate, I Found a Higher Power

After going through what felt like an awful lot of red tape for a receptionist position, I quickly learned why everything was so unforthcoming. I had to sign my life away in anonymity and confidentiality because of the tenants that I now had access to. That ominous job posting turned out to be the most unsuspecting and rewarding job I'd had to date.

It was an incredible, small, and intimate team, and unbeknownst to me, the late nights at airport commission meetings and proofreading complicated legal documents would come in handy when I found myself in New York a few years down the road.

The number of experiences I had for the first time that year, is mind-boggling to think about. I rode in a helicopter for the first time. I declined being pimped out to a city official. I got to plan a lavish birthday party with full access to a waterfront Malibu home. I listened to spine-shivering moments of history recorded on someone's voicemail. I was the pit bull and first line of defense against any shenanigans that walked in off the street.

I was great at this job because I could not feel starstruck by who walked through the door. So much so that I laid the pit bull on thick for a very, very, very well-known movie producer, while my boss laughed because I had no idea who he was. There have not been many experiences thus far in my life where I could see that everything had in fact happened for a reason. I famously have said on many occasions that "Everything happens for a reason; you just haven't seen it yet." In this case, I can see so very clearly why everything happened the way that it did and why I ended up in that job.

I learned a very simple and valuable lesson about money at this job. Being young, wild, and free in Los Angeles, we are often saturated with what "having money" looks like. To me, that looked like fancy cars, bottle service at the clubs, gorgeous girls, and sleazy guys. That's how I viewed "having money in LA" before this job. While this is clearly an overgeneralization, and recognizably not applicable to everyone, what I learned in this job about money is this: If you have real money - like a shit ton, never be able to spend it all in your lifetime, kinda money - one would never know by looking at you. This image of flashy, sexy, lust-filled extravagance wasn't real money. That was show money. That was play money.

My entire perception of what it meant to have money changed. The people that I met with the most money I had ever personally spoken to in my real life, were some of the most laid back, casual, normal people I had ever met. They dressed like normal people. They acted like normal people. Sure, they had kick-ass cars and toys, but they treated me like a normal person. They never acted as if they were better than me. This is an experience forever ingrained in my memory. My goals for wealth changed instantly. I pray to God that when I have *that* much money, I am still a humble and grateful human being.

The second important reason this job was so divinely guided was that two of the five people that I worked with would change my life in a very unexpected way. At this point, it had been a little over a year and a half since I had stopped drinking. One day, while in the office,

I was stewing in some madness over something that probably wasn't important, and these two were leaning against the counter over my desk. One of them asked me, "Are you sober or just not drinking?" I said I was sober. They looked at each other in a way that seemed to complete a conversation I was not privy to.

One of them handed me a blue book and said, "Read this. Look for the similarities and not the differences." Taking the book in hand, I agreed.

I got home from the gym that night and cracked open the book I was given. I am not one to turn away a personal recommendation for knowledge, so I dove in. Seemingly able to set aside any preconceived notions, I read on and on into the night. I got to a chapter that talked about sex and stopped in my tracks. I closed the book and called my coworker.

"I understand now. I'm an alcoholic," I said.

"Great, I'll pick you up in the morning. We are going to a 7:15 meeting," and that was that.

I walked into the back of a funky Santa Monica coffee shop to find a room lined with chairs, and a table on the small stage at the front of the room. I smiled awkwardly at the overly enthusiastic greeters standing in the doorway, then I sat down and heard exactly what I needed to hear.

I heard a man share about how he was losing his mind over something, and his significant other had calmly grabbed him by the shoulders, looked him square in the eyes, and told him to go to a meeting. My heart sank. What was this place?! I had never felt so seen. To this day, that is the type of relationship that I strive for - a partner who sees and understands me so clearly that they will put aside their desires to fix my problems and shoot it to me straight - someone who will send me to a meeting. I had never felt like I belonged anywhere in my life as I did at that moment, in the back of that funky cafe, amongst that group of total strangers.

After the meeting ended, everyone hugged and laughed. It was as if they were all friends. I didn't understand it then. The two men who had stood over my desk the day before, now stood beside me as folks began to bustle. They told me that I needed to find a sponsor. To find a woman who had what I wanted. They introduced me to a few lovely ladies who were all very adamant about exchanging phone numbers.

Just then, I felt a tug on my arm.

Her! They pointed. She is a badass, you need a hard ass like her! They introduced me. "I'm hard too," I thought to myself, "I'm sure we will get along swimmingly."

She handed me her card and said, "Call me every morning for thirty days and we will talk. If I don't answer, leave a message. Get comfortable developing a relationship with my voicemail and I will call you back after I get settled into work." So I did. And she did. And just like that, she became my sponsor.

As I sat down on her couch for the very first time, I handed her a list of all the people who had harmed me. I took it upon myself to get started in advance. She smiled and said, "We will start on page one. Actually on the inside cover." She took me through every word of that blue book and taught me the things she knew as they were taught to her. She was by the book, and she was hardcore. I instantly felt scooped up into her arms and her home, and given a safe space to grow, and love, and feel all of my feelings.

She is one of the primary reasons that I was able to even be cracked open to feel any feelings. Before her, I lived a firm "fuck your feelings" motto for many, many years. She cracked me wide open and devoted herself to my wellbeing every day since that first day in the cafe. To this day, as I type this with tears of gratitude running down my face, she is still my sponsor and a trusted and very cherished member of my life.

She took my hand when I was completely broken and has never let go. Still to this day, I am forever grateful for that job I took in total desperation for being the catalyst that led me to her. She has loved me through my absolute best and my darkest of dark, dark days. That still isn't even the last "everything happens for a reason" that came out of that job, but one day at a time.

I have no idea how I survived a year and a half before ever getting into a 12 Step program, but I highly advise against following in my footsteps. I white-knuckled it for a year and a half and couldn't ever figure out what was wrong with me. I had stopped drinking, so why didn't I feel better?!

This program first taught me that I had a problem and that my life had become unmanageable. But have you met me?! I am so organized and well managed! I was sorely mistaken. And all those "problems" that weren't magically resolved after I cut the booze? Yea, that is the unmanageability they spoke of.

Then came the kicker, I was told that I was insane and that only something greater than myself could restore me to sanity. That right there was one of the things that had kept me out of the program all that time. I didn't want any part of the bible-thumping cult. I was better off on my own, where no one judgmental being was going to tell me what to do or how to believe. To my surprise, as I began to delve into my studies, I found out that this could not have been further from the truth. The text was actually quite humble and very clear that its creators knew only a little, and that the actions they set down were merely suggestions. No one was ever trying to force anything down my throat. Ever. I could get behind that kind of humility.

I resonate so deeply with the acceptance that the authors knew they didn't have all the answers. I heard them saying that we are just doing the best that we could, and here was what we have been doing. Never ever since that first meeting in the funky westside cafe have I ever felt like God or religion were forced upon me. Had that been the case, I probably wouldn't have stayed.

I could admit that my life had become unmanageable and that I was mildly insane, but I grew up repelling organized religion, so I was stumped. I believed in science and the universe, but I couldn't believe that a guy standing at the front of the church was the sole messenger of God and everything he said was the truth. That just wasn't my jam.

Back on my sponsor's couch, she asked me one day, "Can you believe that I believe?"

"Sure!" I said.

"Great," my sponsor responded, "You can have my God until you find one of your own understanding." Thank you, I think?

The next suggestion was to decide to turn everything over to the care of unknown greatness, as I understood them. (WHOA! Insert mind-blowing emojis) As I understood them, that is what my sponsor meant when she told me that I could borrow her God for the interim. She explained to me the word "G - O - D" as just a convenient placeholder. It does not mean that you have to believe in any particular religious God. She taught me from the beginning that I didn't have to understand it and that I could call it whatever I was most comfortable with. I chose to call my great unknown, my Higher Power.

I am a pretty self-sufficient gal, so the notion of turning my will and my life over to anyone else, God or not, was not my idea of a good time. I like to be in control. I like to know all the details. I do not like surprises. I want to know of all things before I commit to anything. One could say, I might be a little bit of a control freak.

Coming up in the program on the westside of Los Angeles, I heard everything under the sun described as people's Higher Powers. I heard everything from the doorknob of the meeting room to the universe, to a Mickey Mouse phone, to the ocean, you name it - I've heard it. Another reason I am eternally grateful for coming up in LA, I was *never* the weirdest person in the room. While exploring and trying on ideas of what my Higher Power could be, with not much avail, my sponsor sent me to the beach.

She told me to stand at the edge of the water and try to control the waves. I could not. I was, however, now very wet. The simplicity of my damp jeans brought me back to right-sized. There was nothing, I mean absolutely nothing in my human power that could control those waves. At that moment, I understood. I didn't know what to call it, how to explain it, what/who it was, but I understood.

After that experience at the beach, and still unable to explain or name it, my sponsor put me on my knees, and together we prayed a prayer that resulted in a "white light experience" that people often speak of when they meet God for the first time. It wasn't just the first time I had ever willingly gotten on my knees to pray, but it was also the first time that I ever intentionally spoke to a power greater than myself. And low and behold, they responded.

I still get teary-eyed when I playback that first prayer on my knees. It was a profound spiritual experience, and I can take myself back there like it was yesterday. It was at that moment that I knew I was not running the show. I had been trying for a long time, but I was merely an actor. I was given the answer to my problems, and I felt so much pain and misery because I was still trying to run the show. That is not my job.

August 17, 2015 - the day of that first prayer on my knees - I gave my Higher Power back control of the reins.

Riding that pink cloud, my sponsor told me, "Everything you put before God you are guaranteed to lose." I heard the words she spoke to me, but I didn't hear her.

18

Guilt, Shame + Remorse

As I dove deeper into my program, I felt a sense of belonging. I felt this sense of "being home" that I hadn't felt in my life since long before my social conditioning had begun. I sat among humans who were nothing like me. They did not look like me, they did not dress like me, they had very different life experiences than me, but there was one huge common denominator that made a soul connection within me. The way these people spoke about the pain inside of them resonated so deeply within me that I knew I had found my people.

In all the counseling that I had done throughout my life, I had never felt as seen and as understood as I did when I sat in those rooms. The more I began to resonate there, the more confusing my life outside seemed to become. At the time, I was dating a man I was wildly in love with. He was much older, and emphatically into me. However, the more time I spent inside of the rooms, the more uncomfortable he became. I was beginning to change, and he could not stand the commitment I had made to my program. My schedule was no longer as flexible, my meetings became nonnegotiable, and I was spending a lot more time with my sponsor. He was losing his grip on me, and his discomfort quickly shifted into insecurity and anger. This was the first of many signs that my life was changing.

He became needier and would often show up at my apartment unannounced with flowers. He even tried to get me to skip my Sunday morning meetings to have brunch together. When I continued to prioritize my meetings over our time together, the gestures of his affection began to increase. One evening over dinner, as my lease was coming up for renewal, he asked me to move in with him. Completely caught off guard, I almost choked on my food. Flattered and distracted by the infatuation, I considered his proposal with enthusiasm.

But when I drove home that night, no longer in his presence, I found this familiar knot of discomfort in my belly. It was sharp and almost nauseating. I didn't know what it meant, or what to do with it, but I noticed that it only happened when we were apart. I questioned the pain. I wanted to know if this was my body showing me how much I missed him while we were away. I questioned if moving in together would eliminate this feeling.

He worked in television production and had a very routine life and schedule. He was Mr. Responsible, and Mr. Predictable, at least most of the time.

One day, when we had planned to have a day date, he just didn't show up. He had been acting strangely for days, being short when we spoke on the phone, and spending a lot of extra time at the gym. When I was finally able to get a hold of him that day, he sounded completely wasted. It was in the middle of the day for god's sake! But then again, who was I to judge? His gym time was usually incredibly regimented, and the drinking in the middle of the day was very new behavior.

He swore that he had overslept and went to the gym without even realizing we had plans for the day. He insisted that I come over and let him make it up to me. I knew that meant 'take me to dinner,' and an evening full of delicious sex. I hung up the phone, sat in my driveway, and fumed, then finally made my way to The Valley. But I knew the sex would make all of these feelings go away.

He pulled me onto the couch when I arrived and started kissing me. He tasted so heavily of liquor that I couldn't even stand to be that close to his face. Every neurotransmitter in my brain began firing, like this wave of psychosis overcame me in an instant. Pissed that he had lied to me about being at the gym when he had clearly been at the bar all morning, I told him to fuck off and left. I was out the door before he could even say a word. Pulling out of his neighborhood, my car drove me on autopilot back to the westside, straight to a bar I knew on Wilshire Blvd. Before I realized where I was driving, I found myself sitting in the parking lot behind the bar. With every fiber of my being, I was ready to drink.

I was *so* angry! I wasn't just angry at the fact that he had stood me up, but more so at the fact that the taste of alcohol was so prevalent in his mouth as we made out that I spiraled into this psychosis of lunacy, ready to drive off the deep end into a bottle of tequila. It was the first time since I stopped drinking that the obsession had total and complete control of me again.

"Now what was I supposed to do with all these feelings?" I thought to myself as I sat in the bar parking lot. I clearly wasn't going to get to fuck them away today as I'd planned. I so desperately wanted to cry, but nothing came out. The moments that followed are blurry. I was in a complete red zone. No ability to act, speak, or think, just pure fury and rage.

My car started and I drove home. To this day, I do not remember starting the car. I do not remember driving home. I do not recall anything from those moments other than the fact that I ended up back at my house and not on a bar stool with a drink in my hand.

By the time I arrived home and sat on my bed, I had messages and messages from him raging about how much I'd changed, how my 12

Step program was the devil's work, and I was guilty of drinking the Kool-Aid. It was at that moment, listening to all of his messages, that I had a deep knowing inside of me again. I broke up with him right then and there.

I'd love to say that things got better from there, but that was not the case. My sponsor began having me work on my personal inventories. I was first tasked with looking at my resentments. That would be easy, I had a lot of those.

What I didn't yet understand about the personal transformation process was that our experiences with others are just mirrors. And the real work begins when we can look at ourselves honestly and see our part. As it would turn out, some years later, this is some of my favorite work to do with others in my transformation coaching business. Here's the thing about this work - we must be willing. We must be completely willing to go to any lengths to get to the root of how we operate.

When I first sat down to begin this work, I was willing! I had plenty of resentments. I was able to get clear on what I was resentful about, why I was resentful, and how it was affecting my life. I dove all in, put pen to paper, worked, worked, worked, and then one day just didn't. I would say that I got busy, but that isn't even true. I got distracted. To take it a step further, I would say that I forced myself to find distractions.

The guy I had just broken up with wouldn't take no for an answer. He was not willing to accept the breakup. He was challenging my boundaries! I didn't know how many other ways of "we are broken up" I could use to get him to leave me alone, but it was exhausting.

At the same time, I took on some side work that I was able to do in my downtime, while at the office. Being an expert accountability partner and creator of a mean color-coded spreadsheet, I began getting offers to help other people break away from their full-time gigs and become independent. I had been successful at restructuring and organizing other people's businesses so that they could scale and grow in their zones of genius, and the word was getting around.

Unbeknownst to me at the time, as I was collecting and organizing incoming media data, I was managing the sponsor deliverables for a motorsport racing series. The information didn't matter to me, I was just good at receiving, organizing, and redistributing, so I got paid to keep doing it. I did such a great job that in the spring I was offered an opportunity to join the gal I was working for at the first live event for the racing series. I said yes!

And that's how I attended my first ever motorsports event just outside of Dallas, Texas. The first time I heard the trucks hit the track I was in the trailer banging on keys. The sound of trucks roaring stimulated something inside of me that I had never felt before. My eyes must have become the size of my head because the other gals I was working with said, "Oh yea, you've never been to something like this before!" We stopped what we were doing, and they dragged me out of the trailer. I pressed my face against the fence, mud bombs flying past my head, and the sound of adrenaline racing past my ears. I felt like a kid on Christmas morning. The giddiness was undeniable within my body.

"This was awesome!" We didn't grow up going off-roading like a lot of other families in Arizona, we spent all of our time traveling to Southern California for soccer tournaments. Fueled by dirt, fossil fuels, and adrenaline, I was hooked.

After that weekend, I was offered an opportunity to work full-time as an event producer for the race series. I went back into the office the next week and gave my notice. I was goin' on the road!

And just like that, my life got big, and the importance of my inner work got small. That's like hitting a grand slam out of the park, at the bottom of the ninth when your team needs one run to win, and you stop at third base. You wouldn't stop at third base when your coach is telling you to run home and win it all. That is where I got to in the work, I hit a home run and then plopped my happy ass on third base because ... Something shiny!

19

Making it in a Man's World

Life on the road quickly proved to be my dream life. It was intoxicating, it was exhilarating, it was just grimy enough and wild enough, and I traveled a ton - often weeks at a time. It also was far enough away from my ex-boyfriend whom I finally had to threaten with a restraining order. Being on the road was a great, big, sexy distraction!

I received a crash course on working a program of recovery from a distance, and how to navigate the waters of attending mandatory after-parties every weekend. Thankfully, my sponsor has the grace and patience of a saint! What I wasn't prepared for was the obsession of that "boy crazy queen" award popping up again. I had been online dating regularly in my sobriety, but nothing prepared me for my first summer on the road.

One of my very first friends on the road was a man named Mark. Mark had been in the industry for a while and was brilliant. We worked fairly intimately together in our small traveling circus, and as we spent a lot of time together, I quickly learned how to navigate his flirtatious personality. Mark took me under his wing and taught me a lot that year. To this day, I am extremely grateful that he was my first friend in this wild new world.

Of course, it was not long before the flirting heated up and we started sleeping together. Our flirtation extended beyond our road warrior adventures and leaked back into real life. I brought out something exciting and sexy in him. We had grand dreams of being together, traveling together, and all the things! Just as soon as he fully left his wife, of course.

I trusted Mark, and he was so crazy about me, so I believed him when he said he and his wife were separated and were just cohabitating for the children. I hadn't yet learned how incestuous this industry was. My heart literally shattered the first time I met his wife and saw how in love with him she was. I buried myself back in my work and would never let anyone know how devastated I was. We never slept together again, no matter how drunk and flirtatious his tantrums would get. I am an "all in" or "all-out" kinda girl and serial dating was never my jam. My walls were back up, and I was all out. I knew I was never going to let another man play me that way again.

The more time I spent on the road, the clearer it became that this 'man's world' needed to be run by women. This industry was the epitome of the masculine patriarchy[6] that is unbearably common in the United States. It was so disorganized, so slimy, so self-seeking, and so dysfunctional, it was like a train wreck where you just can't look away! As Queen of the color-coded spreadsheets, it was no surprise that I excelled quickly in my new endeavors. I was now producing for two companies, back-to-back, overlapping all summer, with the same skeleton crew. We were a little roadshow bopping around between these two traveling circuses, and suddenly half the monkeys became my responsibility.

Being a young, confident woman who had built a career on getting to the inner truths of another's intentions, I quickly learned the two primary motivators for guys who worked on the road two-thirds of the year: beer and sex. While not to imply I was having raunchy sex with everyone that I needed something from, I did however have no moral issue with driving my golf cart around in the middle of the night, dropping off bribery beers to motivate the guys to push from hour twelve to hour fifteen of work. Neither of these jobs was a particularly high-end gig. Our higher-ups often promised the highest intentions, without the budget to back it up. Our job was to produce a champagne experience on a Kool-Aid budget. Simply put, our job was to make the impossible possible. To our detriment, we got really good at it.

As we got proficient at managing the traveling circus, I got proficient at proving my authority in order to get things done. I learned just the right way to wear my eye makeup, and just the right way to giggle and smile to get anything I needed to get done. I was quite surprised by how easy it was to be successful in this man's world. I had all the right assets.

20

I Met My Match

Innocently sitting on the floor, cross-legged with my laptop, working through a staff meeting in Fort Lauderdale, my life was about to change in a way that I would not fully be able to grasp for many years. With multiple unsuccessful attempts to recreate an experience so intense, I am going to share a poem that I wrote, entitled "Fort Lauderdale," which I feel perfectly embodies this experience.

FORT LAUDERDALE

THE SOUNDS OF THE ROOM VANISHED.

EVERYTHING SUDDENLY A BLUR.

THE SOUND OF MASCULINE CHATTER IN THE HALLWAY DRAWS UP

MY GAZE.

MMMM...

THAT VOICE.

MY SENSES BEGIN TO TUNNEL TOWARD THE DOORWAY.

THOSE ARMS...

STILL SEATED ON THE FLOOR, LAPTOP IN HAND

BUT SOMEHOW NO LONGER CONNECTED TO MY BODY.

I AM PULLED EFFORTLESSLY ACROSS THE ROOM.

THAT SMILE...

FUCK! HE MADE EYE CONTACT.

MY THROAT DROPS INTO MY PUSSY.

DON'T LOOK UP.

DON'T LOOK UP.

MY EYES REFUSE TO REMAIN ON THE FLOOR.

I HAVE NO CONTROL OVER MY BODY...

AS IF WATCHING MYSELF FROM THE THIRD PERSON

MY EYES SLOWLY MAKE THEIR WAY UP YOUR CALVES...

THAT CHEST...

THOSE SHOULDERS...

THAT SMIRK...

THOSE EYES...

FUCK!

THOSE EYES... I SAID DON'T MAKE EYE CONTACT!

PIERCING. JUST PIERCING.

I CAN DO NOTHING TO PULL AWAY.

WHY WILL YOU NOT FREE ME FROM YOUR GAZE?

I BLINK SLOWLY BACK TO THE FLOOR.

FLUTTERING BACK UP TO YOUR EYES

STILL FIXATED DEEP INTO MINE.

FIXATED + FIERCE

YOU HAVE ME COMPLETELY.

I DON'T EVEN KNOW WHO YOU ARE.

Later that weekend, shortly after the intensity of the office trailer on the water, I found myself back on land, under the awning of the staff hauler, refilling the ice cooler. Bent over, restocking the excessive amount of sponsored energy drinks we all consumed every day, my body jolted in ecstasy. Every neurotransmitter within my being was firing at that single moment. My body was completely unable to produce a breath, as a set of masculine hands gripped firmly onto my hips.

"I saved your life!" he whispered. It was him, the dreamboat from the hallway. Still completely unable to gain control over what was happening inside of my body, and my panties, I gasped, speechless. I turned around to find his face directly across from mine, close enough to inhale his breath into mine. My body softened at the sight of his smile, then melted into complete surrender of his control at the sight of his gaze.

"Who ARE you?!" I screamed inside.

Never in my life had I ever been so entranced by someone's energy. His presence made me defenseless and sedated, while simultaneously emphatically aroused. Nothing else in the world mattered that weekend, I had to know him.

Being in charge of delegating staff meals, I made sure to hand-deliver the meals to his crew that day. His gaze was just as piercing through his sunglasses as I pulled up next to him. If the lady boner in my pants could talk, I wouldn't even tell you what she'd say! He had a hex over me, and I had no intention of fighting off this witchcraft.

Also conveniently in charge of staff communication, I didn't have to search very far for his phone number. I played it coy as I sent him a text message about his lunch. It was on! My enthusiasm for my work just seemed to get in the way of daydreaming about that sexy man across the track. I found every excuse to talk to him that I could, including plopping right down next to him as he finished his staff meeting, and demanding that he tell me about the sleeve of tattoos that graced his voluptuous arm.

He reveled in my attention, and it was not long before we were texting back and forth all day, every day. Everything about him fascinated me, and his flattery and impression of me never fell short of exceptional. The way he paid attention when I spoke, the way he made eye contact deep into my soul, and the way he engaged with me, were a girl's wet dreams. But that wasn't even the best of it!

He challenged me in a way that no man had ever done before. He was intellectually stimulating and not afraid to call me out on my shit. I am a Gemini through and through, so to me, mental connection with someone is one of the sexiest things on the planet! He quickly came to know me even better than I knew myself and easily became my best friend. I didn't even stand a fighting chance; I was crazy about him. I was all in, and I was addicted. We fell emphatically head over heels in love, and fast! His name was Liam.

To say that Liam and I had a steamy love affair would be the understatement of the century. It was the best summer of my life! He empowered me in ways I didn't even know were possible. One of my favorite things was the way that he would explain how impressed he was with my work.

"I've been in this industry for twenty years, you're the real deal. You'll run this shit someday, no doubt!" was a normal validation of my work. Damn, did he make me feel jubilated and elated! Sure, it was stroking my ego, but I loved the affection and attention. I was undoubtedly infatuated with this man.

However, it wasn't just about me. I completely melted his tough-guy exterior, and he poured his whole vulnerable heart to me regularly. He was going through a lot in his personal life, an ugly divorce, troubled teens at home, and I was the only support system that he had. Keeping our steamy relationship on the down-low from most coworkers, my newly found depth of orgasms really brightened up my ability to thrive at work. I was on cloud nine and Liam was my everything. I had the dope job, constant travel schedule, and the sexiest man in the paddock, my life was good!

Liam had been in the industry almost as long as I was alive at that point, so he was a great sounding board for my frustrations with the systems and management of these gigs. And he always held space for me to vent, release my feelings, and then fuck them all away. He reminded me of how incredible I was at my job and that I would run these companies one day. It's almost like he had a crystal ball that I didn't have access to. Remember how my sponsor told me that anything I put before God I was guaranteed to lose? Yea, I didn't remember either, until it ran me over with a pickup truck.

There was one event that year that I did not produce. I opted out so I could attend my brother's graduation from college. While I was away traveling with my family, Liam brought his kids to the historic site that we were producing an event for. His ex-wife came too. Liam was a ghost that entire weekend, making no mention that the children's mom was in attendance. I heard about her presence at the event from one of my coworkers, while I was helping them troubleshoot a work issue. The man I was head over heels in love with was radio silent in the same hotel as his ex-wife. I like to think that I am a creative genius with a great imagination, so it came as no surprise that I drew up some elaborate stories about what was going on in my absence.

I confronted him about it the following weekend when I returned to work. He was acting differently and something in him had shifted. He wouldn't elaborate about what had happened and I was livid. As the end of the weekend drew near, he left the job site without even saying goodbye. He got in his truck and started across the state, heading home. Watching him drive away, he couldn't have brushed me off in a way that was any more obvious as I called him to see what had happened. He was not interested in explaining.

"Who the fuck does this guy think he is?!" I raged to myself, "Just peace out without so much as a goodbye?!" I was beside myself, blood completely boiling inside of me. How was I supposed to function after feeling like I had just gotten run over by a bus? I had no idea, but my boss was messaging me to get back to the hauler and help her wrap up the event. Unsure that I was even still able to breathe, I made my way back to my computer. I wasn't about to get into this with her, so I took a deep breath and sat down next to her.

I went back to banging on keys and completely shut down emotionally. We had just produced one of the most perfect events of the year, and my walls were thoroughly back up. He had royally fucked up. In true Morgan fashion, I had to lock it all up and get back to work. There was no time for emotion when there was this much work to be done. So I didn't. I buried myself back in my work and pretended Liam never existed.

21

The System is Broken

As I sat next to my boss under the hauler on a quiet post-event afternoon, just after Liam departed from my life, a forklift slowly drove across the front of our tables. Hanging on to the side of the forklift, Miss America waving at us, was one of the Jasons. The other Jason was operating the forklift, cigarette hanging from his fingertips, also Miss America waving at us. Looking up from our laptops, Amy and I burst into laughter! Enjoying the unexpected jolt of positive emotions, I softened back into my work.

"Oh, My God!" Amy exploded, as she whacked me on the side of my arm. Knowing nothing, to my knowledge, of my steamy romance with Liam, she exclaimed, "Oh My God! You need to date Jason!" as she continued to hit my arm with the back of her hand.

"He is the nicest guy I know, and he is divorced from his wife," she explained enthusiastically. Never really taking any time to get to know him since he joined the squad mid-season, I had been otherwise preoccupied much of the year.

"You need to flirt with him tonight at the afterparty! You need to make this happen!" Amy declared. Her sense of certainty was strangely intriguing. As I gazed across the paddock at the Jasons, now off on their smoke break, all I could muster to myself was, "Maybe she was right."

With the pain of Liam's absence already locked up deep within me, I put on an extra layer of confidence that night as I got ready for the afterparty. Whatever swag and confidence I decided to show up with must have worked because two other guys who had tried to get my attention all summer were layin' it on thick that night. Leaned up against the bar, I looked completely past them as they spoke. My attention was scanning the sea of eager to unwind mechanics and operators. I finally spotted him. In all normal accounts and circumstances, the tattooed mechanic from Huntington Beach would have made the most logical choice to get over my broken heart, but I thanked him for chatting and beelined for Jason.

There were a handful of other staff members that had joined midseason with Jason, so I took this opportunity to plop down on the couch in the middle of their clique. I made eye contact, batted my eyelashes in all the right ways, and let the games begin. I was feeling sexy and confident. He seemed surprised by my directed flirtation, as did the woman who was so used to having her drinks bought by him. There was an awkward get-to-know-each-other period where she lingered in the conversation, hoping I was going to move on. I did not.

Before leaving the bar that night, we had exchanged phone numbers, and by the time I was back at my hotel room, he had texted an invitation for dinner the following night. I have no idea what it was about Jason that night at the afterparty that made me so interested in accepting his invitation. I don't know if it was the fact that he was the furthest thing from my type, or that I knew he was legitimately not married, or the fact that another woman was seeking his attention that night. Either way, I found myself very interested, and I graciously accepted.

I was pleasantly surprised by Jason at dinner that night. He was very engaging and forthcoming with me. He was entrepreneurially inclined, having owned his own business for almost twenty years before getting into motorsports some years ago. He was significantly older than I was, so we communicated in person and on the phone much more than we communicated through text messages. That was refreshing to me as well. It was surprisingly comfortable to let Jason in that way, and so quickly, and I seemed to have completely forgotten about Liam.

As the season progressed, Jason received an offer to manage a very prestigious concert at an extremely high-end event at the end of the summer. He began to spend full-time status in another state and was no longer traveling with our little pop-up circus. Then one afternoon, he called me nervously and invited me to join him in Texas on my off days, explaining that this was the biggest production he had ever managed alone, and he needed the sense of calm and serenity that I seemed to bring him. He told me that I could stay with him, have full use of his car, and work from wherever I needed to be, as long as he could see me when he got off work.

This felt like the most grown-up request I had ever received, and I had no idea how to respond to him, especially since we hadn't even slept together yet. It was all so new, but I felt intrigued. After much deliberation with my sponsor, I accepted his invitation, and he flew me out to Texas.

Before my big adventure in Texas, I made a pitstop in Arizona to see my tattoo artist. We had a session on the books before Jason's offer had arrived, and I have never been one to miss an opportunity to sit with my favorite artist on the planet! We had a full-day session planned, so it was a perfect pitstop to make along the way.

Catching wind that I was in town, I received word from Liam who happened to live in the same city as my tattoo artist. He knew I was pissed, and he was ready to explain himself. Still, completely in the dark about what had shifted in him, I invited him over to see me while I was in town.

Liam knew nothing about Jason, so he engulfed me in his scrumptious chest before he was even halfway through the door. I fit so perfectly in his man nook. He started to profusely apologize for upsetting me and finally explained himself. But before we could finish the conversation about how his ex-wife was making his divorce hell, we were already entangled in a mixture of ecstasy and manipulation. Fuck! He knew exactly how to turn me on. By the end of my stay, and countless hours of mind-blowing lays later, I knew this was goodbye for real.

I was going off to Texas to see if there was potential with Jason, and Liam was considering trying things one more time with his ex. As I boarded the plane to Texas, I left all feelings for Liam behind. I wanted nothing to do with him if he was going to choose that woman over me. I was done. I cried silently the entire way to Texas.

I arrived in The Lone Star State where Jason poured out his gratitude for me coming to visit. He was kind and very appreciative of my moral support. He opened up to me on that trip and I liked that. The more time we spent together, the more I grew fond of Jason. It wasn't a love-at-first-sight kind of situation, but we grew to be incredible partners and friends. We could talk about anything and often spent our days working and daydreaming about how we could run these companies better ourselves. I had a blast supporting him in Texas and will never forget the intensity of the breached security entrance just before we had finished setting the ultra-high-end VIP seating in front of the concert stage. There's a special bond that forms when you go through the trenches with someone in that way. It was a very positive experience being there with Jason.

After wrapping up in Texas, new luxury cowboy boots in hand, we made our way to Las Vegas for the season finale of the race season.

I could barely stand to be within a hundred feet of Liam that weekend, but he was there, nonetheless. The weekend was a blur of thunderstorms, lightning, evacuations, and nightclub invitations to meet the National Anthem singer whom I had booked. That was also the first time that I learned how bartenders are supposed to use different glasses for nonalcoholic drinks.

It was late after the first night of our doubleheader event weekend and a bunch of us had gathered in the casino to blow off some steam. I was helping hand out drinks from the bar and grabbed my club soda and lime from the bartender. Everyone was deliriously cheers-ing away a wildly stressful day, as I took a giant slug from my straw. My body revolted as I swallowed my drink! My tongue was on fire, my arms were tingling, and I was instantly sweating. I had just discovered that there was vodka in my soda water.

Seeing the pale sweaty glaze over my face, Jason caught my gaze and asked if I was okay. "I can't breathe, I need to get some air," I said as I rushed past him. As I gasped for air, leaving the smokey casino doors, I hysterically started to cry. Half hyperventilating, half compulsively shaking, I pulled my phone out of my pocket and dialed my sponsor.

She didn't answer. I called her again. She didn't answer. Fuck!

It was 2:30 in the morning, what the hell was I supposed to do now?! As sheer panic began to set in, my fingers dialed my old coworker. He answered. Thank God!

"Morgan, breathe," he said, "It's okay. You're okay. This was an accident. These things happen!" I was unable to speak, so he kept talking.

"Morgan, listen to me," he said, "This was an accident, and the only thing that matters now is what you do next." Nodding as if he could see me, I saw Jason exit the casino doors near me.

"Morgan, depending on what you do next, this is not breaking your sobriety! I need you to understand me," he said again. "Go back to your room and get in the shower. Let it all out and call your sponsor again first thing in the morning. I promise you; you will be okay."

I believed him.

Thank God he had answered the phone. I can honestly say that I don't know that I would have been able to stay sober after that night had he not picked up the phone!

Hanging up the phone as Jason reached me, I melted to the ground crying. Jason wrapped his arms around me as I balled on the concrete stairs of the hotel. Between sobs, I tried to explain what just happened. Receiving enough of the gist, Jason went back inside, gathered my things, and helped me up to my room. As instructed, I washed away the day and fell face-first on my bed. What a horrific way to end an uber exhausting day.

The next morning, the sun came out and cars were back on track. It was the final round of the season. My sponsor assured me that I was in fact alright, and I got back to work. The storm had passed, and all was right in the world again.

As we wrapped an incredible season, an afterparty for the books, I got in my car to drive back to LA. From his explanation later, Jason watched me drive away from the Las Vegas strip and knew he wasn't willing to let me go. Shortly after returning to my apartment in Los Angeles, Jason asked me to be his girlfriend. I was fairly used to having long-distance relationships in between events, so I accepted.

Summer was long over, and the ocean breeze began to change with the time. Only back in my apartment for a few days, Jason called with a wild idea.

"Come to the Midwest," he said. "Spend the off-season here with me."

And just like that, Jason asked me to move in with him. Having only spent forty whole days in my apartment that year, I broke my lease and packed up what would fit in my car. Jason flew to Los Angeles, and we piled into my Elantra. With the rest of my life packed in, Jason and I started on an epic adventure across the country.

After a romantic night on the snowy rim of the Grand Canyon, and a pit stop at Mount Rushmore, we finally found ourselves in the middle of the Midwest in the middle of winter. This girl had a lot to learn about that snow life, seeing as we didn't get much of that in Arizona or SoCal. It was a cozy winter of falling in love and dissecting the nooks and crannies of the jobs we had just finished.

After a lot of napping and very heavy comfort food, we couldn't help but realize how dysfunctional it all was. We spent weeks weighing out the pros and cons together and decided that we were going to go independent and not work for either of those race series the following year. And just like that, we started designing a new life for ourselves, and it was wild how quickly it all manifested. We were determined that there had to be a better way to produce events, and we were going to make it happen. We spent the whole off-season brainstorming, analyzing, consulting with old colleagues, and dreaming up a better way.

That following year, in early spring, I was given the opportunity to sit on a committee for a tourism development meeting in North Carolina. I brought Jason along with me, and together we completely blindsided the board with our new ideas on how to shake up the events they were thinking of funding. We brought a fresh set of eyes to their sleepy little town, as well as a confidence that caused them to hire us on the spot for more consulting opportunities.

Being that this was a government entity that wanted to hire us, we had to abide by very specific business and insurance requirements. To accept the offer, Jason and I had to form a business entity. So we did!

It took longer for us to come up with a business name than it did for me to have us filed with the state and officially open for business. Needless to say, in a matter of days, we had a business entity, a bank account, and a lawyer. We built our entire business plan around taking the dysfunctional, antiquated event model and flipping it on its head. And just like that, Jason and I were in business together.

Once we began working with the Tourism Authority, all the irons we had placed in the fire over winter seemed to start calling. Spring was upon us, and the event industry was awake from its hibernation.

Last year's race series started making phone calls and our old colleagues started calling us to see if we were going to be coming back, to see if we were going to accept their offers. Jason and I held strong in our stance, we were not willing to work under such conditions anymore, and we were forging a new path. We graciously declined, which stirred up quite a bit of gossip and surprise. Less surprising however was that all of our friends had decided to go back. We were the lone wolves, and we were going to make it happen elsewhere. Someway, somehow.

The Tourism Authority reveled in our rebelliousness to traditional antics and kept us busy with development projects and a few new events that we brought into town. In between, Jason had taken a gig to drive transport for a hospitality rig and it wasn't long before I was brought in to manage the catering fiasco no one could seem to get under control. I even did some time, as a trial, with a traveling obstacle course series. When it came time to make me an offer, I was on a flight to meet Jason in Miami before I could finish hanging up the phone to decline. It was just another dysfunctional system just like the ones we had left behind, and I was no longer available for that kind of work. It was not worth the effort and time commitment for that little pay.

Declining their offer cracked open something within me that was very deep-rooted. Jason wasn't involved in that gig at all, and it was the first time that I had stood up for my worth completely on my own. It was one of the harder things I had done, as I loved the product and the people that I had met. Just as I had been, they were all stuck in the hamster wheel of the traveling circus rise and grind. I knew that wasn't a merry-go-round I was willing to hop on again. Yet, I still cried silently from New Jersey to Miami.

Jason was already on site for a job where we were managing the track build. We had carefully written our contract, hand-selected our team, and were doing it all our way! It felt incredible to land onsite to a gig I felt in control of in this way. As I walked into our hotel room in Miami, there was the largest display of sunflowers I've ever laid my eyes on! Beside it was a note that read, "I'm really proud of you. See you at the track." He knew the way to my heart; that was for sure.

And so it was, that Jason and I filled the year with miscellaneous odds and ends, including helping some buddies out at the Final Four basketball tournament, which was way cool for a college basketball nerd like myself! A few weeks after the gig in Miami with the sunflowers, Jason got a phone call that would change everything for us.

The director of events for an international race series called and invited us to her wedding in Spain. She and Jason had become friends at an event, a couple of years prior. I was honored to be included in this intimate ceremony. Jason and I went on to spend a week exploring Barcelona before heading up the coast to the Spanish countryside for this stunning wedding in the hills. I was impressed with how my five years of learning Spanish came right back to me with the right motivation of tapas and paella. OMG, the paella! I still dream about that paella!

The wedding was straight out of a fairy tale, and I fell in love with the bride's Spanish relatives. They were from a region north of the city and were so incredibly welcoming and kind to me. We danced and dined along the wine country of Spain until the wee hours of the morning. I've never been one to shy away from a wedding dance floor, but something about the sexy Spanish air and sangria got my man on the dance floor that night in a way I had never seen before. We fell in love all over again beneath the twinkling patio lights. The people I met, the sunsets I would see, the food we would eat, it truly was a magical occasion! An occasion that would solidify the following phone call we received shortly after their honeymoon.

Sofia called one afternoon, while Jason and I were back home in the Midwest. She had taken some much-needed time off from work and shared all about her honeymoon. I hoped that Jason and I would share in a celebration of our love as beautiful as Sofia's. It was just perfect! We reminisced about her incredible wedding and thanked her again for including us. Then she got down to business. "We are going to produce an event in New York City, and we need your help," she told Jason. No one had ever raced in New York City, so we were intrigued. Sofia went on to tell us that it was already a done deal, there was already a venue scouted and they needed boots on the ground management as soon as possible, because their race series was just about to kick off its international season. Her team would be scattered all over the world and New York needed full-time attention to get things off the ground.

Sofia explained that she wanted our company to manage the project because she was so over the bullshit bureaucracy of working with the other agencies. She wanted this experience to be different. That being said, we were the ones for the job! If we could get to New York for an operations meeting, the job was ours. Jason and I looked at each other over the speakerphone and silently agreed.

A few days later, Jason flew to New York to meet Sofia, the track designer, Raphael, whom we had also met at the wedding, and the CEO of the series. The horror stories I received when he called that night should have been the first sign of red flags. Instead, we painted all those red flags green and took the job. Just like that, we had committed to the craziest project we would ever get ourselves involved in.

22

This Is What I've Trained For

As the skies turned to grey, and the first snowflakes began to fall, we were given the green light to begin building our team. Our Morgan + Jason event management company had just landed the contract to produce the first motorsports event to ever be approved within the five boroughs of New York City. No other racing series had done what we had just signed on to do. The closest anyone else had gotten was across the river in New Jersey. Our client was *not* interested in Jersey, it was New York or Bust!

Jason and I spent countless snowy days and hours around our wooden dining room table creating staffing plans, build-schedule drafts and hotel contracts. With very little information yet approved, we moved forward as if nothing in the world could stop us. Our confidence quickly proved to be infectious. The ball was rolling, and nothing was going to get in our way. Every other race series had failed to breach the boroughs, but we were going to make the impossible possible.

We began making regular trips to New York, meeting with the European operations team for site recce, and beginning conversations with the mayor's office and with local authorities. All of those airport commission meetings I was forced to attend in Santa Monica suddenly became useful! I was also incredibly grateful for the much tinier scale opportunities that I had received while speaking at the

Tourism Authority meetings in North Carolina. While Jason did most of the speaking in New York, I soaked up every word and began organizing the world's largest spreadsheet tracker for our event operations plan. No joke, I literally broke Google Sheets one day and was told I had hit the cell limit for a single spreadsheet. This was a new level of spreadsheet crack; thankfully, I was so organized!

We sat at a conference table every month with the heads of all major NYC departments: Fire, Police, Counterterrorism, Sanitation, Transportation, Port Authority, The Mayor's Office - you name it, we had their business cards. Meeting once a month, we got very familiar with this cast of characters and what was needed of us to play in this sandbox. Jason fit in easily, and they accepted him almost immediately. He was about the same age as a lot of the highest-ranking officials, he was poised when he spoke, and could indirectly answer any questions that were asked of him. When he stood up in front of a group of authorities, he was good!

I, on the other hand, found myself in a very similar situation as I had most of my life: I was much younger than most of the authorities in the room, I was a woman, and I was partnered with a man in a collared shirt. I was always spoken to second, I was always bypassed for clarification on a question, and I was often completely ignored. Lucky for me, *this is what I've trained for!*

I had spent most of my teenage and young adult life learning how to be taken seriously while being the youngest person in the room and, much of my adult career, learning to be taken seriously in male-dominated industries. Those were both two very different things, but I would need all the tools in my toolbox for this one!

I was a sponge. I did not speak unless I had something intelligent and certain to contribute. I was more organized than anyone in the room, so I was always prepared when someone lacked the information or couldn't find what they were looking for. I saw and absorbed every word of every conversation. My wildly wicked processor of a Gemini mind was on full-speed 24/7. To be taken seriously I had to be as smart as a whip, and I knew it.

As the months passed, we began to bring our core operations team into the city meetings. When the women on my team spoke, the questions would be readdressed to Jason. There was only one woman in those meetings that could control that room, and she knew how to lay it on thick. The senior authorities in the room seemed to be used to working with her because when she spoke, they listened!

The fight for my voice was not a fight I was interested in pursuing in those meetings. All that mattered was getting what we needed for the event to continue moving forward. I understood the game, prepare the men with all the tools they needed, let them speak, and receive the approvals that we needed. I knew my place, and I played my role.

Once we got back to our side of the bridge from Manhattan, I knew I could settle back into being myself. I was the mama bear, and the well-being of my people was among my top priorities. I knew that if I continued to empower the people around me that we would indeed be able to make the impossible possible. Immune to the weather as winter storms came and went, we were still onsite hosting civil works meetings at the Piers week after week. And as the sun began to crack through the permanence of grey skies over Brooklyn, we met the change of the seasons with our biggest meeting of the year. It was time to submit our permit packet to the city.

And by permit packet, I mean a ten-pound binder, holding over 600 pages of operations plans. It was the most impressive piece of organizational collaboration I had ever seen. When I plopped the binder on the conference table, the authorities all told us that our operations plan was larger than the one they used for New Year's Eve on Times Square and significantly larger than the one used when the most prestigious football game comes to town. The look on their faces was almost comical. That alone confirmed our success and authority to be doing what we were doing. Additionally, the content of that massive binder was more detailed than any of the authorities even cared to look at, let alone process. It was almost as if they had tasked us with such insanity just to test our willingness to even show up that far. Regardless, we blew them away.

Receiving the permit approval was the major hurdle we needed to accomplish to get to work - or so we thought! We would soon come to learn, over and over again, that the more we dug into this project, the more layers of fuckery we would have to dig through.

The racetrack we were going to build spanned across three Port Authority piers. This meant that it wasn't City property per se, but the politics and bureaucracy were so thick between the City and the Port Authority that alone spread thicker than our entire job site. Every conversation was completely contradictory, we were to undo everything we just promised to those people, in order to please the other people. It was an entangled mess of manipulation and just all-around debauchery.

To build our racetrack across the middle pier, we had to displace thirty-six businesses that operated within the pier and its warehouses. From trucking companies, to produce distribution, to event furniture rentals, to city-appointed construction companies, these were not small operations that we would be disturbing, but we agreed to find suitable options for every single business.

The displacement of the pier businesses became a full-time job within itself, so we flew in the most patient man we knew to specifically manage the relationships with those business owners. The hunt was on for surrounding properties to house these operations and shit was about to get weird.

As we began to Google Earth the neighborhood, we had no idea how intimate this community was. We found that when we started making phone calls to inquire about properties and vacant lots in the neighborhood, people already knew who we were. And I don't mean, "Oh are you those idiots who think you're going to produce a race through our neighborhood?" I mean like knowing where we were from and about Jason's children. We usually met in abandoned warehouses, and there were often men watching us from inside their cars while we met with property owners. As outsiders, clearly not from around there, scouring the neighborhood got sketchy real fast!

Luckily for us, Jason's magical power is making influential people instantly love him and want to be his friend. The deeper we got into conversations about temporarily leasing these properties, the sketchier the conversations became. And the more we were able to meet their asinine requests, the closer Jason became to some of the major players in the neighborhood. Everything I'd ever heard about Brooklyn seemed to be true - the corruption, the manipulation, the quiet intimacy of the neighborhood. We were getting deeper into the weeds of the community, and I feared we would never make it out, or worse we'd end up in the river like the body and floating head I had seen at the end of the block.

There were deals involving large sums of cash in duffle bags, there were conversations that our lawyer told us to never tell him about, there were even threats of "a new pair-a-boots"[7] late one evening in a parking lot on the river. Those bodies I had seen clearly hadn't received the concrete boots, since they had floated up down the river near us. There was no doubt that we were in the thick of it, and we had some major ass-kissing to do. And we did.

There was blackmail. There was conniving. There were back door deals that I will take to my grave. It was not even uncommon for there to be black cars slowly pulling up next to us on the job site and a driver saying, "Get in" through a crack in the window. There was one ominous "get in" experience where Jason was gone for more than four hours! It was one of those situations where I didn't know who could be trusted, who was working with who, or which way was rightly up. So I held my breath for four hours straight, trying to keep my team moving along, all while hoping that Jason was okay.

After a long day on site, Jason and I would often burn the midnight oil, strategizing for the following day's meetings, and unwinding from the insanity the day had brought. When we needed to get creative to break through a barrier at hand, we would climb the ladder to the rooftop and pull out a pack of smokes. I would hop onto the old chimney well, letting my legs dangle below me, and Jason would pace the rooftop, silently taking in the first few drags of his cigarette.

Burning through a few cigarettes on the roof of Jason's apartment one night, we agreed to what would become our Brooklyn Code. We agreed that we would do what we needed to do to get this job done, as long as we always listened to our intuition. Up until that moment, we already had more than a handful of experiences that we knew were not safe or far too illegal to touch and had luckily listened to our gut and walked away. We agreed that we could push the boundaries of our ethics to the very brink of crossing the line, as long as we always talked each situation through honestly and openly together, knew we would always have each other's backs no matter what, and knew each other's life insurance plans should anything go seriously wrong.

Jason and I were 'ride or die.' We were a great fucking team! The code was set, the irons were in the fire, and we knew that together we could handle anything. We never shared that conversation with our team, or clients, or our lawyer, but we knew what we had to do. It was common for us to exit a room to go for "a deal" together, which was code for smoking a cigarette and talking through our boundaries with the situation at hand. Our team knew these moments to be serious Mommy + Daddy time and that we would come back to them when we had a plan.

And push our boundaries we did! No matter how sketchy things got, no matter how insane the ask from the client was, no matter how much money we had to pull out in cash, Jason and I could get through anything together. We were a powerhouse couple and powerhouse leaders who had secret weapons that will forever live on those apartment rooftops and between our cum stained sheets.

We did our best work together in the middle of the night, or amongst the brisk fog of the early morning air. We could sit out on the chimney well on the rooftop and overlook the entire city. With the Statue of Liberty to the left and lower Manhattan to the right, we did our greatest and deepest growth right there on that rooftop. Brilliant ideas swirling about with the smoke of our menthols billowing around us. He made my skin thicker and my ability to manifest any idea into reality constantly empowered his confidence. He knew that any situation he talked himself into we could climb on that rooftop and figure it out together. I was his voice of reason and sounding board, the barometer gauge of where we stood on the pressure of the thread of our boundaries.

No matter how vulnerable we had to get together to decide our next course of action, we always walked away confidently and in alignment with where we were going. The people around us saw none of that deep work together, only the confidence and alignment we exuded when walking into a room together to discuss our next plan.

We grew and we were tried. We met adversity and we overcame. We were threatened and we prevailed. Together, we were a perfect team with perfect harmony. He was the face, and I was the anchor.

We figured out the heartbeat between us and exactly how to never skip a beat. If he was ever in hot water, like the night when he was being baited into a fistfight on the river, I would have him defused before anyone else realized what was going on. The team went about their work, and we had our secret code and our closed-door Brooklyn life. We were good.

23

The Crumbling

As the spring air began to thicken and the humidity began to rise, the core team and I were now living full-time in Brooklyn. Counting down the days to the displacement of the pier tenants, the in-depth civil works, repaving, and the start of the track build, we were starting to find our groove. As the old saying goes, we were becoming a well-oiled machine.

The thing about it though was that the better things got in New York the further I got from my program and my step work with my sponsor. Still sitting on that fourth step, I wasn't willing to look at my personal inventories when life was going so well. I was figuring out how to play the roles that I needed to play in New York. I was also figuring out how to play all the roles that I needed to play to have a thriving business and juicy relationship with Jason. It was all coming together!

Don't get me wrong, it wasn't like I forgot about the step work that I was supposed to be doing. I thought about it every day and, every single day, I chose to shift my attention elsewhere. I clearly wasn't willing. I was making more money than I ever had in my life, I was in complete control of my schedule, and I had a gorgeous modern apartment walking distance to the job site. I was much more willing to continue to build this big, beautiful, bicoastal life instead. So I did.

My life on the road was manifesting into something from a fairy tale. My parents were super proud of me, all of my dad's friends were super jealous of my lifestyle, and I was finally feeling that success I had been craving for so long. I was finally making it as a successful woman in this fucked up man's world.

As that New York summer melted on, more people began to join us onsite. We were managing a full-blown event, and it was all happening! From track build to grandstands, to VIP hospitalities, and even displacing the pier tenants, it was *all* happening. The weird part of it all, however, was that the more comfortable and successful I felt, the more I could see the light fading from Jason's eyes.

I'd always heard a saying in the industry that said, 'you sell a little bit of your soul for every live event that you produce.' I assumed that this was the point in the operation that the soul-sucking began to happen for Jason. He always looked exhausted, he was hardly eating, and he stopped joining in team gatherings. It was almost as if I watched the bags under his eyes grow in overnight.

I noticed a shift at home as well. He wasn't interested in our usual late-night manifestations to change the world. He was no longer very affectionate towards me, and to be honest, he used to not be able to keep his hands or his mind off of me. I would lay down next to him every night and just like that he couldn't have been further away. Every night for almost two years we would fall asleep holding hands, and suddenly there was a palpable divide in our bed. The kisses were hollow, and the sex was as empty as his eyes. I assumed my thoughts were correct, the event was getting the best of him, and his soul was slowly seeping away.

Over the next few weeks, I found myself having to pick up the slack in our business. Not only were we producing this event, but we still owned our business. Staff and vendors needed to be paid. Our clients needed to be babysat and chased down for every invoice we were owed. There were a lot of hats to wear, but I knew that if I didn't do it, it wouldn't get done. So I accepted Jason's situation and went about my business juggling Event Production, CEO, CFO, Mama Bear, Staffing Coordinator, and Emotional Support Animal for the man I loved. "This is what I trained for," became a very common mantra as I transitioned from black coffee to lattes, to energy drinks, to espresso on the rocks.

Thank god for my brilliant assistant who could practically read my mind at that point. She kept me fed, caffeinated, collected, and positive. The truth is, there is not enough gratitude I can express for that angel in my life. She was recommended to me by the local Chamber of Commerce while I was hunting for interns and, from the very first interview in what would become our very favorite coffee shop, we were two peas in a pod. The weeks, months, and years ahead would not have been possible to survive without her. She stood by my side through the highest highs and the lowest lows of what was coming. I can see today how divinely selected she was for me.

As we began counting down to event day, it dawned on me that this was really going to happen! I would jump out of bed in the mornings, get my espresso going on the stove, and put on my power mascara. I woke up giddy every single day and would fall into nothing shy of complete and absolute exhaustion every single night. It was awesome! We were going to pull this off!!

We were so deep in event mode that I didn't even have time to notice how far away Jason was drifting. I had way too many other irons in the fire, and he just buried himself in his work. Most days we didn't even walk to work together because I was off in excitement, and he couldn't be bothered by that type of vibe.

I was walking from our apartment a couple of days before the event, having just had my morning wellness shot of juice, my bags all packed, struttin' down the main street of our neighborhood when my skin got all clammy. I crossed the street just as I did every morning, and I suddenly couldn't feel my feet. I looked down to find myself drenched in sweat and unable to feel my legs. As I began to poke my thighs, my bags fell to the ground as I realized that I couldn't feel my fingers either. I tried to pick up my bag and I couldn't. The air around me instantly got thicker. My hair was now covered in sweat, and I was choking on my breath. I mustered myself to the bus stop bench and managed to pull my phone out of my pocket and dial for Jason.

He finally answered on the second try and was just getting out of the shower. As I was explaining what was happening, I started to completely melt down in panic and tears. What was happening to me? Jason told me that I had probably put too much cayenne in my juice and that I would be fine by the time I got to the office aircon. Sitting completely alone, in the middle of the morning, having a full-blown freak-out on the bus stop bench, Jason told me to find my way back to my feet, keep making my way to the office, and he would be there in a bit. I asked him to please come and help me and he told me I was fine.

I contemplated calling for an ambulance, but Jason had assured me that I was okay. I sat on the bench for a few more breaths and used my useless hands to wipe away my tears. I managed to sling my bag across my body, and by the grace of God made my way to the office. In the five to eight minutes between the bus stop bench and the job site, something in me had shifted. The waterworks were gone, and I had all of my hats out ready to party. My need for success, to be taken seriously, to prove my worth, and to pull off this event were the only priorities. To this day I still don't know if I was having a panic attack, a heart attack, or completely made the whole thing up, but regardless I pushed it all away and never told a soul. I was not about to draw attention to myself when we were about to pull off a historic event like this.

And a historic event it was. We did it! The job site passed the counterterrorism inspection, the track build was perfect, we didn't sleep for days, and racecars were on track! I will never forget that first moment, standing on the bleachers, just before the very first practice, watching the first cars pull out of the paddock. As each car made its way to turn one, more tears welled up in my eyes. By the time they passed me, standing in the VIP grandstand at turn two, my hands were over my mouth in prayer as tears completely poured down my face. I was speechless. It was the most touching moment I could dream of. Looking up at the sky, the Statue of Liberty just across the river, the sound of tires squealing in the distance, I let out a gasping and soft laughter. We had done it! Cars were on track! This wasn't just a historic moment for motorsports, it was a historic moment for New York. The impossible was unfolding right before my very eyes.

The weekend was incredible. Excited fans filled the venue, VIPs drank their way through the bubbles and grub, and there were two epic races. Best of all, the money shot was perfect on the television broadcast! Lady Liberty and lower Manhattan watched over us as the podium champagne sprays matched the fire department boat water show. It was the most perfect weekend, and our client was thrilled. I am grateful that, even in his distance, Jason had advised me to stop at some point over the weekend and just let myself take it all in. I did and it was perfect. I soaked up every moment, we did it! We had made the impossible possible. This inaugural event would forever go down in history.

Luckily for us, this was the season finale for our client, so as soon as we completed the teardown, they all went on holiday. That meant we had five minutes to breathe before they were ready to start working on next year's event. We celebrated with our team and then tore it all down. Even as I type this, it still feels as magical as it did that very first time that I watched the cars on track during that very first practice in New York. We did a really big thing, and it was a really big deal. As the saying goes, "If you can make it in New York, you can make it anywhere." I had made it!

As the celebrations continued, Jason and I hopped on a flight out of JFK heading to our reward vacation together. After a combination of napping and being too excited to sleep, we landed in the Bahamas. I had booked us an uber private house on the perfect pink sandy beach! We were in paradise, and I was on top of the world. Yet I couldn't help but hear my sponsor's voice inside my head, "Anything you put before your program, you are guaranteed to lose."

After getting settled into our house, I found Jason propped up in a chair on the porch. Obstructing his view of the ocean, I bent down to kiss him. I was on top of the world. My kisses grew more passionate as I began to undress him. By the time I had his pants unbuttoned I had his full attention. He kissed me back as he lifted me off his lap and pinned me against the porch railing. We made out for a few minutes before he turned me around and bent me over the railing. This was the sexiest moment of my life! The view, the high, the perfect paradise hideout. I had made it.

In that exact moment, my real-life fantasy popped. He stopped. Before I could understand what was happening, I felt him a million miles away. I turned around to find his eyes completely glazed over, and his body no longer interested in mine. I got on my knees knowing exactly how to rectify the situation, but there was nothing. He was completely uninterested in continuing to fuck me.

As he sat back down in his chair, I could tell that he was not on this pink sandy beach with me. I put my panties back on and tried to brighten up the conversation. I had brewed up some ideas for fun things we could do with his kids when we got home, and as the thoughts finished leaving my lips, he was already freaking out at me. I had no idea what was happening, but we just went from paradise fucking to full mental breakdown in all of about three minutes. He did his best to explain, but none of the words coming out of his mouth made any sense. All I could gather was that he just wanted to be at home. I tried to redirect the conversation back to his children and he raised his voice at me again. What the actual fuck was going on?!

He then explained that he wanted to be at home with his children alone. I confirmed that what he was saying was that he didn't want to be there with me. With his confirmation, I asked if he wanted to be there with someone else? He confirmed.

I was speechless. I was speechless and flabbergasted. We were on the most perfect beach in the world, having just completed the biggest accomplishment of our careers, and he couldn't so much as stand to be around me, let alone fuck me?! He told me that he wanted to be with someone else.

I remember his face perfectly at that moment; exhausted, hollow, moping, and completely on another planet. I vividly remember thinking what a broken shell of a human sat before me. The sacred bond between us had long been broken. I stormed off to the bathroom and melted into the back of the door, silently bawling my eyes out.

As if breaking up with the man of my dreams, within the first twenty-four hours of my dream vacation wasn't bad enough, we were slapped across the face with an even bigger tragedy! Urgent alarms were screaming, telling us to vacate the island. There was a hurricane coming, and it was heading straight for us! Making my way back to the porch where he last touched me, I could see the storm brewing in the distance. The sky looked terrifying, and I knew this was not a drill. Fight or Flight was undoubtedly activated, and I was on the mad dash to get us off this island. Frantically scouring the internet, while on the phone with our travel agent, I scored two seats on the second to last flight off the island. Our tickets were booked, and my world was in shambles. With no time to even process the breakup, we were literally trying to outrun a hurricane.

Unable to make it back to Miami, as everything was already shut down on account of the storm, I found the last available hotel room in Fort Lauderdale. One last hotel room, with one king-sized bed. With literally no other options for miles and miles, Jason and I had to stay the night together one last time, while we tried to get the hell out of Florida. I booked him a flight back home and I caught a flight out west. We were done and I was going back to California.

Catching wind that our vacation had been cut short, work began calling and was coming in hot. The event in New York was such a success that we were immediately signed on to get to work on the next year's event. With absolutely zero time to process what had just happened with Jason, we were on a flight to Europe to get back to work. You could have cut the tension between us with an eyelash. Shit got weird and it was no secret. There were snide remarks openly back and forth at the dinner table with our team, and we couldn't agree on any plan to save our lives. I was sure as hell not going to let this stand in the way of my career, so I locked it all up again and got back to work.

This was the cycle. This was the way that the current system worked. This patriarchy of the American Dream insisted that to succeed in business was the only option there was for success in life. "Fuck your feelings," it said, "as long as you work your ass off to make a butt load of money, you will be happy." I built my entire life on achieving this goal, so why the hell was I so unhappy?

That winter was a blur of chaos. Jason had some intense family issues coming up, our clients were more demanding than ever, his health was deteriorating before my eyes as the stress grew worse and worse, and I was drowning trying to keep it all together. It was a rollercoaster of drama, and in the pits of his despair, he tried to resign eleven times that winter. I wouldn't let him, of course. Every time he would call me wanting to quit, I did what I had been trained to do; I talked him off the ledge. I reminded him why we were doing all of this and slapped him on the ass to keep going.

24

Willing to See Things Differently

Unable to process any of my own emotions, mainly because I was trying to convince the world that I didn't have any, I called Liam. As he shared with me that things hadn't worked out with his ex-wife, again, I knew that he would know how to make me feel better. Liam always did know all the ways to make me feel better!

With every word of affirmation that he spoke, I grew more turned on. He told me that Jason never deserved me, that we had accomplished something that no one else had ever done, and that I didn't need him anyway. He told me that I was robbed of my well-deserved vacation, and I needed to get out of town. Explaining that there was no way I could find the time, he damn near challenged me that I wouldn't do it. That night, while on the phone with him, hell-bent on proving him wrong, I booked a flight to Greece. I was going, and no one was going to ruin this for me. I flew myself to the land of my people, and I hid alone for ten days. It was the first time I had traveled internationally alone, but I heard Sofia's voice in my head. She was reminding me of a conversation we had had about women traveling alone, that I was smart and could fit in anywhere.

There was nothing sexier in Greece than sitting in my rooftop bathtub, smoking my cigarettes, overlooking the Acropolis - that is until I met George in Santorini. George met me as I arrived from my airport transfer and carried my bags down the winding cliffs of Oia. He was very charming, and I loved the way my name rolled off his tongue. As he escorted me to my villa on the cliff, he wished me well and hoped to see me around. And see me around he did. Every time I would venture out on the secluded streets of Santorini, I seemed to run into George. He explained that winters were very slow on the island since the winds made it less enjoyable for the tourists. I didn't mind one bit! I was just happy to be away from everything back home.

Making friends with the locals everywhere I went, I took their recommendation for the best sunset views on the island. Thinking it a smart idea to timelapse video this world-renowned sunset, I soon remembered George's comments about the winter winds. As my feet hung off the edge of the cliff, dropping hundreds of feet into the sea, I gripped my phone for dear life as I watched a boat come in with the perfectly timed sunset behind it. My hair now in a giant rat's nest, face completely windburned, I felt my body let out a full breath for the first time in months. I immediately fell in love with Santorini.

Making my way back to my villa, I ran into my new pal George, who invited me up to the rooftops for some wine after dinner. Not willing to get into the sobriety conversation, I giddily accepted his invitation and made my way back to my villa. As my phone connected back to the Wi-Fi in my room, the dings began blowing up messages and emails from Jason.

Completely unwilling to let me have this time off, he had committed us to completing a major proposal while I was away. Before I knew it, dusk had turned into dark as I was engulfed in attempting to calm the storms back home. Once I finally came up for air, only because I was about to pee myself, I realized I had worked through dinner and could already hear George chatting with every passerby on the roof. I went out for a smoke and couldn't get myself to say hello. I had so much work left to do, and it wasn't worth fighting with Jason about why I needed this time to myself. So I had another cigarette for dinner and cracked open my laptop instead of whatever steamy evening I could have had among the Santorini rooftops. Man, what a cockblock!

That would become the usual tone of things moving forward. Work dominated everything and I was growing increasingly unable to keep my mouth shut with Jason's rollercoaster of emotions. One minute he wanted me back, the next he wanted to let it all burn to the ground. It was exhausting, and it went on this way for months. I wasn't going to let him ruin everything we had built. We had a huge meeting coming up in Miami, and I needed to get my head right. So I flew to Arizona to see Liam.

As always, Liam knew exactly how to pinpoint whatever it was that I needed and deliver. If I needed romance, he would dress me up to wine and dine me with the best of them. If I needed affection, he would sit behind me and rub my back while I worked. If I needed to process, he would hold my hand silently on a walk around the block. If I had some big feelings, he would fuck them away until I couldn't think straight. He was perfect and everything I needed. Everything I needed for the weekend. Then, as he always did, he left and went back to his life, and I went about mine.

Almost like clockwork, moments after Liam left my hotel room, I received a phone call from Jason. He was calling to inform me that he would not be going to Miami with me the next day.

"I'm sorry, what?!" I asked.

"I'm not getting on the plane, Morgan."

"Is this a joke?! This meeting is going to set us up for the next ten years, what the fuck do you mean you're not getting on the air-plane?" I asked. I stopped listening to his responses and I put my foot down. I told him that we were not going to tarnish our reputation and not show up because he was having a tantrum. I told him that we could sort through whatever his issue was when we got to Miami, but he was going.

"Your assistant is already on her way to Florida!" I said, "I don't care what you need to do to get your ass on that airplane tomorrow morning, but you're fucking going."

We hung up the phone and I truly had no idea if he was going to show up. I pulled out my hidden pack of smokes, and I called Liam. He assured me that I would be great with or without Jason. While I appreciated his vote of confidence in me, deep down inside I knew that I couldn't yet do it without him. I knew that Jason still held some of the keys to the kingdom and I wasn't willing to let them go. I wasn't about to let him bring it all down now, so I braced myself for the fight.

Jason arrived in Miami, and I could feel a war brewing. He sat down across from me at the bar table and just stared at me. He said he didn't want to get into it right now, since Ellie was about to arrive. Just then my phone rang, it was Ellie, Jason's right-hand gal. She had been massively delayed all day and still wasn't slotted to be in Miami for another four hours. Jason lost his excuse. Before I hung up the phone, he was already taking back his second glass of wine. This was not going to be good.

I insisted that we go back to our condo to speak in private since this was gearing up to be a hot one. Back in our condo, we agreed to reconvene in five minutes to talk. I went and collected myself in mine, while he retreated to his room. I don't remember many of the details of those next three hours, but it was the only time in three years that we ever raised our voices at each other that way. I am not a fighter; I am a communicator, and he was not having it. I called a time out to go to the bathroom and told him I would meet him outside for a smoke when I was done. We weren't making any headway with the current approach.

I was already working on my second cigarette by the time Jason joined me on the terrace. His energy had shifted. He inhaled that first drag as if he had just finished a wild night of sex. He looked at me silently.

Halfway through his cigarette, he broke his silence, "Seeing you fight with me like that really turned me on."

He went on to tell me that if this business were to dissolve, he hoped I would not be a pushover and that I would fight him tooth and nail like I had that night. I could not have been more disgusted. Ellie had landed and was on her way to us, so I finished my cigarette and contemplated my next moves.

"If we land this meeting tomorrow, the valuation of our company will skyrocket," I said to Jason. "Show up for this and get through this next New York event with me, then you can fucking walk. I won't stop you anymore. You can have your fight."

He agreed.

Ellie arrived and all was back to normal. I knew my code and I knew exactly what I needed to do. The next morning, while getting ready for our meeting at the Miami Boat Show, I asked Ellie if I could borrow some of her clothes. I told her that this meeting was really important, and I needed to shake things up. She dressed me in a strappy top, allowing all my tattoos to see the light of day, and a pair of striped pants that made my ass look amazing! I was *not* about to be hidden in the background this time.

Just as I expected, Jason couldn't keep his hands off of me. It was working. He was drooling and I laid the charm on thick with everyone else we met. He was losing his mind! Once he started hitting the bar at every stop, Ellie finally figured out what was going on. She asked if things had finally exploded, and I let her know that World War 3 popped off in the Highrise before she arrived last night.

She said, "I don't even want to know, but whatever you're doing, it's working. You're running the show now and he can't focus on anything else besides your ass in those pants."

Ellie and I had a great time in Miami and were able to accomplish a lot that week. We met with tequila distributors and high-end executives at swanky bars. It was clear that Jason and I were through, and as my confidence rose like the Miami heat, I knew this was no longer a partnership. One of us was gonna have to go, and it wasn't about to be me.

Back in New York, I had schemed up a surprise for Liam. His son helped me get all of the travel details on the down-low and I booked him a surprise vacation to meet me in the city. He had always wanted to visit New York, and it was my turn to show up for him in a special way, as he always did for me.

It was days before his arrival and another World War was heating up with Jason. I reminded him that we made it through Miami and now we had a couple of months left together in New York and that was it. Then he was free to leave.

Based on his text messages to me, while I was cleaning up my Brooklyn apartment in anticipation of Liam's arrival, my Spidey senses started to tingle. Jason wasn't set to arrive in New York until Monday, which would give me a few days alone to play with Liam. I felt sick to my stomach, especially since I got the sense that Jason was about to sabotage New York. No, not just my weekend 'sexcapades' with Liam, but our baby - the event.

I tried to follow the drunken stream of consciousness on the other end of the phone, and I knew it wasn't good. That voice inside my gut was screaming at me, Jason was brewing a way to fuck me over with the New York event. Fuck that! He was not going to ruin this for me. If he wants to fight for everything when it's all said and done that's fine, but we had a deal. We were both finishing this second year in New York and not going to jeopardize the future of our company, regardless of if we wanted to kill each other or not.

Without skipping a beat, I knew exactly what I had to do. I called Jason and I laid it on thick. I knew he was drinking, and I knew exactly what to say to make him want me. So I did.

I had a choice to make, and it took me all of one millisecond to make it. I was going to sleep with Jason and take back control. I canceled Liam's trip the night before he departed, and Jason flew in that very night. I regretted my decision the second I had made it, but I chose to follow through with it anyway. I had to save my business.

I told Liam the truth, well most of it, and he said that he understood. I crushed him. This was my big chance to show up for Liam the same way that he had always shown up for me when I needed him, and I had crushed him. I chose to save my business.

Jason landed in New York shortly after I got off the phone with Liam and I did what I had to do. The second his taxi dropped him off at my door, I knew it was on. Before he could even take his shoes off, I fucked him like I'd never fucked him before. I took my power back, and he didn't stand a chance against me anymore. This was my sandbox now. He could come along or not; I knew this was all going to be mine.

For the second year's event in New York, I was the head of operations, this was the role that Jason had played last year. I knew that if I could get through this event and show everyone that I could do just as well as Jason, then I would have the respect of the people I needed. I would have the keys to the kingdom.

Whatever energy shifted in me the night I fucked Jason had worked. I had this no-bullshit boss babe energy about me that felt freaking good. It felt so sexy to not walk in the shadow of a man. I showed up to do a job that summer and I did it. I knew when to be charming, and I knew when to be stern. I knew I had mastered the role that I needed to play in New York, and it felt damn good.

All cocky attitudes aside, I still never broke my Brooklyn code I had made with Jason. I always had his back and I always talked through every financial decision that we had to make. If the client ever pushed back, Jason assured me that he handled it with Sofia, and I was clear to move forward. No matter what shit was happening between us, I did not fuck around with the code of our business.

The operations side of the event was solid. We had made some pretty significant changes since the first event, but I felt like I handled the new opportunities. But something else was going on in the business side of things; the finances were not making sense. I had received the funds from the client to pay our vendors, but nothing was adding up. I was literally watching money pour out of our bank account that neither Jason nor I had authorized. Our bank account was being hacked. I sat at my desk one steamy afternoon on the phone with the bank, watching thousands and thousands of dollars draining from our bank account right before my very eyes. That is quite possibly the worst thing that could happen in the middle of an event.

The paperwork was a nightmare, and because I handled most of the financial transactions for the business, I was the only one who could come up with the answers to the questions as quickly as the bank needed them. We were being shut down and rebooted right in the middle of our event. Every time the controller and I would get a handle on things, more fraudulent checks would hit the account. It was a nightmare, and I was burning in hell. Alone, I was literally burning in hell. Alone.

I was drowning and Jason was nowhere to be found.

The client started to get testy, and I was not about to let any of this blowback on our team. So, I put on my big girl panties and kept plugging away. Head of operations by day, everything else in the shallow breaths in between.

I somehow made it to the end of that event, the second success in the books. I felt like the significance bucket in my life was overflowing, and yet, somehow there wasn't that same magic this time. So much of that last month was a blur, but the things that stuck out were adventures nonetheless - like walking out of the bank with a backpack full of cash, so I could stash it in my apartment to make sure that we could make payroll and it wouldn't vanish with everything else. Additionally, I vividly remember being on the phone with Jason, tears streaming down my face, just begging him to have my back and help me get through this nightmare. He agreed and then proceeded to go radio silent.

I knew that if I didn't book my flight out of there, I would be stuck in Brooklyn resolving this financial crisis for months. Jason had already left town, it was just me, my assistant, and the controller left. I booked my flight to Italy and told Jason that I would work my ass off until then and then I was out. I was taking my holiday alone, and he would have to take over from there.

The view of the city the day I flew out of New York couldn't have been more bittersweet. I could literally see the ghost of our racetrack and it made me want to vomit. The finances were still a nightmare and vendors were ready to be paid. Jason had to hold it down for a couple of weeks so I could decompress. But I must have miscommunicated the duration of my holiday because my phone was blowing up within a matter of days. Jason couldn't figure out how to access my documents and he didn't know where to find this or that. You would think it was the first time he had ever tried to access our business systems. It may have been. Either way, the drama followed me to Italy.

I called my sponsor as I left town and she reminded me to hold on to my ass. "In this program, we are taught to save our asses, not our faces," she loved to tell me.

I thought about picking up my step work while I was in Italy, but my priority was *pasta!* Adventuring from the prestigious Lake Como to Venice, to the Italian countryside, to the fishing villages of Cinque Terre, to Sienna, Florence, and Rome, I dove in hard into the Italian culture. My priorities consisted of carbs, espresso, cigarettes, and gelato. Italy was phenomenal and I felt deeply connected to the band of misfits who had come before me. The Great Masters, writers, painters, and visionaries. Italy made me feel absolutely alive. Completely alive, that is until I checked my phone. Jason was going bananas about me leaving the country at a time like this, and it took everything in me not to laugh. Welcome to the party dude!

I was so adamant about avoiding him while I was away that I even dove back into my step work. I will never forget this one defining moment in Venice. I was having dinner on the water, after having treated myself to the most stunning Tiffany's necklace, finally beginning to feel like I could breathe again. I was watching the gondolas bring in gorgeous couple after gorgeous couple, while I sat working on my sex inventory while awaiting my pasta. It was at that moment, mere hours after paying cash at Tiffany's, sitting on the patio of a waterfront hotel in Italy, watching the passion and love on people's faces as they completed their gondola rides, that it hit me - I was so deeply sad and alone.

I was in one of the most romantic cities in the world, rewarding myself with a well-deserved break, with a notebook in front of me of all the people that I had harmed. I lit a cigarette and stared across the crystal water. I hadn't been willing to pick up this notebook all this time because I wasn't ready to be done playing the victim. In order to keep moving through my fourth step, I had to get honest about my part in all of this. I had a few more cigarettes and devoured my pasta. Politely declining the dessert wine, I ordered an espresso and got back to writing. I moved right to the inventory about Jason.

I had so much anger directed towards him, but you'd never know it flipping through my notebook. We were so happy and in love the last time that I picked it up. I could hear my sponsor's voice in my head, I knew I had to start with him. I moved through my inventory on Jason and moved right into Liam. Holy hell, I was such a piece of shit.

I saw it right there, in black and white, in my handwriting, all of the harm that I had caused. I didn't have it in me to move on. Unsure of how to process the harm I had caused Jason but seeing what I had written about Liam damn near broke my heart in an instant. I made my way back up to my room and cried myself to sleep. By crying myself to sleep, I mean I laid in my bed crying for hours because I had an Italian espresso after dinner like an idiot. I was wide awake until 4:30 in the morning that night. Lesson learned, no more espresso after lunch.

I couldn't ignore my phone any longer even though I was desperate to stay in Italy forever. I had to get back to reality. Jason was ready for World War 3.5 by the time I got home, but I just didn't have it in me to fight. We made it through New York, and he was now free to go.

But he didn't go. He bashed me and bashed me for how messed up things got with the finances. I even started getting heat from our client about it as well. Appalled that I could leave the country at a time like this, it all started sounding awfully familiar. I knew in my heart that this wasn't my fault, so I tried to just brush it off and get back to work.

The more the weeks passed, the more tension built with our client. They couldn't understand why "this was the first time they were hearing about this," their favorite saying in the book. I had nothing left to give these people. I told them the same thing that I told Jason, "Here is all of my documentation showing everything I have done, please feel free to offer any support as soon as you'd like." Neither did. Just a constant barrage of Morgan bashing.

As summer turned into fall, I was back in my apartment in Huntington Beach. I spent my days on my porch swing staring at the trees and smoking cigarettes. Most days I couldn't get out of bed before 11:00 a.m., except on those bloody Thursdays when I had a 6:00 a.m. call with Europe. Most weeks I took that call from my bed, with nothing new to report because so many people were still waiting to be paid from our last event. The finances were still in shambles, and we still hadn't received all the money back that was stolen. And yes, I was still being blamed for the entire mess.

A few cigarettes a day soon turned into a few cigarettes per sitting, which turned into complete isolation from anything else in my life. I was living in a $3,000/month condo, exactly one mile from my favorite beach in California, and I was completely and utterly miserable. The guilt, shame, and remorse continued. I was spiraling into a very dark space and there wasn't much I could do to stop it. Even talking to Liam didn't cheer me up anymore. I was hitting my bottom, and that train was haulin' full speed ahead, real fast. I made mention at some point to my best friend, Noel, that I was certain no one would even notice if I was gone. Everyone hated me and was blaming me for all the problems in New York, so what was the point of even living. I had kept to my code and gone to battle to protect my people, and I was left on the firing line all alone, taking round after round after round right to the chest. I was dying a slow and painful death, so just ending it all now seemed like a much better idea.

Noel also happened to be my doctor, so that conversation quickly became a psych eval with her partner. It was mutually decided that my suicidal ideations were cause for concern and they recommended putting me back on antidepressants. I had such deep opposition to prescription drugs after my experiences with them in college, but I did as they suggested and called my sponsor.

My sponsor reminded me, as she had for years, that in addition to our 12 Step programs, sometimes we needed outside help. I knew that some of my very best friends in sobriety needed outside help in the form of drugs and therapy. I never placed judgment toward them, but to me, it felt like a complete and absolute failure. I would much rather die than live with the thought of failing at my businesses.

My sponsor and I both heard those words come out of my mouth and agreed that I would take the pills. So I called Dr. Noel before I could think it over any further and she sent over the prescription.

The pills began to work fairly quickly, which meant that I was pretty neutral and numb most of the time. Navigating these waters was complicated and confusing in my brain. I could still think for myself but felt this constant fuzziness in the space between thought and action. I hated the fog that they caused me, but I felt less like I wanted to die. Now I just constantly felt like I was crawling inside of my skin, which was likely a result of incomplete step-work.

Then God spoke to me one night, in the form of my best friend's husband. He told me point blank how terrified he was for me that I was still sitting on that fourth step after all these years. He told me that was a lot of guilt to be carrying around. He looked me square in the face and for whatever reason, I heard him. I felt his fear for me, and something clicked. Within a month after he told me that, I completed my fourth step, delivered my fifth step with my sponsor, and got right into six, seven, eight, and nine. That's all it took. I will never forget the look on his face, the genuine concern for my wellbeing.

Fall began to turn into winter again and by this time, Jason and I barely ever spoke. Even though the financial situation was still not resolved, the contract had been renewed for New York's third year and we were expected to get back to work. We got the team rolling and I was off to Colorado to help my best friend deliver her second baby. I was part of her birthing plan, and I was not going to miss that for the world. The beautiful thing about the timing of this trip was that the meds made me sick every time I smoked a cigarette, and I wasn't allowed to smoke around the girls in Colorado, which meant it was time to kick the habit. Dr. Noel brought me in for routine labs and a cocktail IV to help me kick the cravings while I was in town.

I didn't have much energy to give, but anything was better than listening to Jason talk about the money drama in New York, so I buried myself in helping Noel prepare the house for the new baby. She got me a pass to her gym, and I found some old friends in the weight room who helped me move some energy around. One afternoon, having just finished my pre-workout as I pulled into the gym, I got the call to head to the hospital. It was time.

Jason called just as I was heading to the hospital. Cracked out on my pre-workout with nowhere to direct all of this energy, his call was the perfect storm waiting to happen. He had called to bitch about something or another and I just couldn't bear the sound of his voice for one more second, so I hung up the phone and called my buddy Daniel. Daniel was the only person who knew the whole truth about everything that had been going on with Jason and I needed to get this one off my chest before I went in to deliver this baby. I arrived at the hospital before Noel and company and started pacing around the parking lot.

Daniel listened to what I had to say and in a very poignant voice that I had yet to ever hear from him, he said, "Morgan, how much more? How much more of this are you going to take from him?"

He continued, "I know you think he is going to be the one to leave but look at what this is doing to you. Look at the dark pits of hell it has taken you to. Morgan, how much more are you going to take?"

His words penetrated the depths of my soul and sobered the pre-workout right out of me.

"I don't know," I softly replied. "I really don't know."

Just then, my very pregnant bestie arrived, and I hung up the phone and witnessed the most beautiful moments of the human experience. But just after participating in the birth of Noel's baby girl, we were immediately met with another form of hell shortly thereafter with Noel having postpartum complications that resulted in an additional six days in the hospital. I stayed by her side every moment of what appeared to be more intense agony than pushing that baby out. Our six days of high-intensity trauma in the hospital were exactly what my body needed to kick that nicotine. Whatever withdrawals I was experiencing meant nothing compared to the pain I felt while watching my best friend and soul sister go through what she was going through.

Once we finally got Noel and the baby back home, I was able to crack open my laptop to check in with the work world. There were dozens of voicemails and messages from Jason demanding that I get back to him and how could I be so off the grid when we clearly discussed what an issue it caused when I left for Italy. I was in the hospital with my best friend, I didn't give a shit how pissed he was at me.

I got on the usual weekly meeting with Europe and was asked to deliver an update on a project that wasn't due until the end of January. I informed the team that there was no progress since most companies were already shutting down for the holidays and each had promised to get back to me after the New Year. As a result, I wasn't expecting much action in these next couple of weeks. My response picked up a vibe from the European crew. One of my teammates called me as soon as we hung up from that call and asked if we had done something wrong. Not to my knowledge, I told her and proceeded to call Jason.

He laid into me before I could even get a word out, about how much I had embarrassed him, what a disaster this cleanup was going to be, blah blah blah. I had *no* idea what he was talking about. "Morgan, you are literally being paid to produce these results before Christmas, what the hell have you been doing?" he said.

"Before Christmas?! Are you insane?! This deadline has been set for the end of January for months. What are you talking about?" I asked.

I hung up the phone and called my teammate back. I didn't tell her anything and just asked her when the deadline was for our procurement information?

"End of January," she responded. I thanked her and called Jason back. As would turn out, Jason had engaged in a conversation with Europe that I was not privy to. During that conversation, he had agreed to move the deadline to December, and yet no one in my department seemed to know about it. He took no responsibility for the lack of communication, and I was beside myself.

By the time I left Noel's house in Colorado and drove to Arizona for Christmas, I felt like an empty shell of a human. I had no physical energy, no mental energy, no cigarettes, and I was so deeply perturbed that I had been set up that way. Everything about this situation with Jason felt premeditated and manipulative. How could we have gotten so far from our ride or die code?

From doing my step work, I had been willing to see my part in it all, but that still didn't excuse the way he was acting. My part aside, I could only see two options at play here. Either he was falling so far off the wagon that he had no idea what he was doing to our business, or he was deliberately manipulating all of these situations as a way to force me out. Either way, none of this felt good to me as his business partner. No longer suicidal on account of the meds, I felt a new emotion come over me as I drove back to California from Arizona. I think I felt sorry for him. I truly felt sorry for Jason if he was that miserable or angry of a person. I knew what it felt like to play in those pits of hell, and I wouldn't wish it upon anyone - even him.

We had a couple of conversations over New Year's because he was pissed that I had turned the heater off in my Brooklyn apartment when I had left town a couple of months ago. He went for New Year's Eve in the city, but his lease was already up, so it was my fault that my apartment was freezing in the middle of winter while I was not there. I just mustered up an eye roll and let it go.

A couple of days after New Year's I woke up out of a dead sleep and sat straight up in my bed. I was wide awake, and out of nowhere I asked myself, "Is there ever going to be a day that he chooses to have my back over saving his face?" The answer 'no' could not have flown out of my mouth any faster. I called Jason and I resigned.

I knew with absolute certainty that that was the truth. I did something I never thought I would be the one to do. I shattered my own damn heart, and he accepted my resignation on the spot. I had finally had enough.

Self-Reflection Opportunity

- What areas of your life do you feel certainty and significance?
- What relationships in your life provide you with validation of your worth?
- Whose opinion do you depend on while making decisions?
- What are your core values?
- Have you ever remained in a situation that no longer made you happy because of guilt or feeling like you shouldn't leave?
- How have you allowed yourself to become someone you didn't like?
- In what areas of your life are you feeling resistance?
- Do you feel that more often than not people have wronged you?
- What big life changes have happened in your world? (i.e. lay-offs, divorce, heartbreak, loss, accidents, injuries)
- Have you read self-help books, or some form of personal development, and put it down before actually completing the work?
- At this point in the book, are you willing to see things differently? (Are you willing to accept there is another option, or do you believe your destiny for suffering is set in stone?)

3

The Phoenix

25

Who the F*ck am I Now?

As I flew back to New York to pack up my apartment, I felt completely hollow and numb inside. It was as if the pain of what I was about to do was too big to process. I knew that I needed to pack up my life in Brooklyn before I told anyone else what I had done, but I had no idea how I was going to be able to break the news to my team. I also knew that I had a lot of legal work ahead of me, and I just couldn't bear to process any of that just yet. I needed this moment to physically close the chapter and get back to my safety net on the west coast before I could even begin any of those logistics.

I arrived at JFK to be punched in the face by New York winter. The winds were howling, the air was freezing, and a snowstorm was on its way. Unbeknownst to me, it was the perfect analogy of the experiences I was walking into. With my best winter coats awaiting me in my apartment, I froze my way to the rental car station across the airport, collected my minivan, and made my way to Brooklyn.

The minivan was both nostalgic and functional. I knew New York was expecting rain and snow while I was moving out, so a pickup truck just seemed like a dismal choice. The comedic relief was that a minivan is always the event production rental of choice. We have to transport a bunch of humans, load it full of miscellaneous things and stuff, and the side door can be opened to facilitate drive-by beer drop-offs for late nights on site. Over the years of working events, I have rented and driven every style and brand of minivan on the market, and some are quite schmancy these days! I will never judge another soccer mom ever again.

When I arrived at my apartment, I cranked up the heater and ordered my favorite emotional support meal in the neighborhood. Then I slowly paced around my apartment while I waited for my mozzarella sticks and Bolognese to arrive. There wasn't a lot of stuff to pack, but I had no idea where to begin, so I found myself standing on my red shag carpet rug in the living room, just staring out the patio windows. I couldn't believe this was the last time I would have this view. I also couldn't believe that I had made the moronic decision to quit smoking before completing this endeavor. I regretted that decision immensely at that moment.

My attention was jolted as the buzzer rang. My dinner had arrived. I had lost all track of time and somehow ended up sitting on the floor with tears rolling down my face. A flood of emotions had crashed over me, and I couldn't believe that I was walking away from everything we had built. This was my baby. This life was my everything. I silently sobbed into my mozzarella sticks as all of the blood, sweat, and tears I had given over the years played through my mind. I felt like I finally understood the analogy of life flashing before your eyes the moment before death as the life I had previously lived replayed before my very eyes.

I couldn't help but feel like I was breaking my own damn heart and that I would come to regret this decision. But I also knew that for now, I had to pack up my things and go home. The integrity in my heart was no longer aligned with the integrity of what was needed from me here. I was so far out of alignment that if breaking my own heart was what needed to be done, then that's all I knew how to do. Begrudgingly moving to the couch, I stared out the

French door balcony as I aimlessly ate my Bolognese. I didn't pack a single thing that night, I just sat there.

The physical task at hand was simple: move the furniture and job materials to our warehouse down the street and pack my personal belongings into the empty suitcases for the trek back across the country. Up until that moment, I had felt very confident in my ability to compartmentalize my emotions from the task at hand. However, this one now felt massive and impossible.

Over the next couple of days, I did everything I could to delay the inevitable. I went through every article of clothing to see if it still sparked joy or if it was going to be donated. That was unsuccessful as everything I touched was now nostalgic and sentimental. Mere moments later I also considered burning it all, and just hopping on the next flight out of town.

As I continued to rustle through my belongings, I found the bag of jewelry and accessories from my 30th birthday party. My best girlfriends and I had enjoyed a "Roaring Twenties" themed weekend in the city the previous summer, and it was necessary to try it all on again! Every pearl and feather took me back to better days of laughter and sunshine. As I snapped selfies in my getup, I realized how long it had been since I was truly happy. Even in all my pearls and accessories, I couldn't help the tears that began to stream down my face. As my throat sank into my belly, I knew it was time to start doing what I came there to do.

Slowly but surely, a few days, a lot of carbs and espresso later, everything had been packed and moved, except my bed and the overstuffed suitcases. My once buzzing Brooklyn apartment was now cold and bare, and I still couldn't help feeling like I was making a huge mistake. With no more delays to be made, I booked the flight home and made my way back to the airport.

Normally religiously requiring an aisle seat, I climbed into my window seat and melted into the support of the window panel. The blustering storm had calmed long enough for the air to clear, but the cool temperature of the window felt soothing to my forehead. As we took off, heightened by claustrophobic anxiety and no clear path to the bathroom, I was calmly reminded of the magic of the window seat. When departing from NYC, from the left side of the plane, on a crisp and perfect dusk evening, you can see the sparkle and detail of every bridge and building in the surrounding boroughs.

I inhaled deeply as I identified Central Park down below me, down to Lower Manhattan, across the Brooklyn Bridge, and right into the neighborhood where I woke up every morning to make the impossible possible. As one lone tear streamed down my face, I could see the entire experience, in one ascending moment, as we climbed to cruising altitude. As the night danced in, and we floated through the clouds, I watched the shine of the city melt away below me.

After making my way back to the left coast, as my little brother likes to call it, I knew it was time to face my decision. I made every effort to not screw anyone over in my departure, so my now ex-boyfriend/ex-business partner, our lawyer, and I developed an extensive transition plan to outline exactly what I was willing to do to soften the blow of my departure. In reality, I was so broken and hurting inside I would have done anything just to make it all end. When it came time to talk about finances, I was so burnt out and miserable that I didn't fight for a dime, I just begged them to let me go. I was not willing to give Jason the satisfaction of fighting with me anymore.

I had such a belittled sense of my worth that I chose to walk away from three businesses, the team I loved and respected to the deepest pits of my soul, and any sense of respect I had for the man I once held in such high regard. I had no idea how to stand up for myself any longer and I had no fight left in me to give. I took what little of my dignity I had left, my savings account, and the promise from my sponsor that I would have a good night's sleep someday very soon, and I walked away from it all.

After four long and painful, unpaid months, I completed the obligations I had outlined in the transition plan. And I was left with a complicated cocktail of relief, rage, feeling broken and exhausted, as I was faced with two very mind-boggling questions: "What the hell am I going to do now?" and "Do I even know who the fuck I am anymore?"

26

Meeting Lady Elton

I received a text message from an old friend one day. She was working at a crystal expo in my area and was reaching out to let me know that she had been watching the woman at the booth across from her and my name kept popping up in her head. She told me about the aura photography the woman was doing and that I needed to come and check it out if I could make it down to the convention center.

Very intrigued by this news and what could possibly go down at a metaphysical expo, I cleared my schedule for the following day. Arriving at the convention center, my brain immediately tried to go into event mode analyzing the egress of the event. I took a couple of deep breaths and reminded myself that that was not why I was there. I was merely a spectator and a guest, and I was in no way liable for the outcome of this function.

As I made my way to my friend's booth, and up and down the convention center aisles, I ogled the jewelry, stones, and gorgeous clothing at every turn, and couldn't help but notice some activations that just had some really funky energy about them. I diverted my eyes, sticking with the "don't make eye contact" method of avoiding getting sucked into unwanted conversation.

The entire hall was quite overstimulating with so many different energies swirling around, but once I turned the corner at my friend's booth, I saw her - the woman doing the aura photos. She was surrounded by a sea of people, and she radiated through all of them. I could only briefly see her face, as the line of people chatted, excited to see her. I turned my attention to meet my friend, who was momentarily free from customers, but I couldn't help but feel my attention being drawn back to the woman across the aisle.

Laughing at my inability to stay present in our conversation, my friend urged me to go get in line. She informed me that the mob of people at her booth was significantly smaller than it had been earlier in the day, so I'd better make my way over to her. Before she could even finish sending me off, I was already on my way to the aura photography booth.

The line moved quickly, and soon it was my turn to have my photo taken. One woman took all of my belongings to the table on the opposite side of the stool, while another woman guided me on where to place my hand. There was a cold metal box to my left, with grooves to place my fingers in. I tucked my palm comfortably into the energy reader sitting beside me and turned my attention to the camera before me.

Less concerned with the chatter around me, I was geeking out at the camera set up in front of me. It looked like an old box camera with a curtain behind it. Pleased with the placement of my hand, the second woman stepped behind the camera and under the curtain. I geeked out so hard inside, what a stunning contraption that was! From where I sat, I could see the mirrors inside the box and assumed it was operating similarly to an old polaroid slide, with a single produced photograph.

The woman peered out from behind the curtain to inform me it was time. I held very still and couldn't help but notice the intensity of my fingers on the cold metal plate beside me. I held my pose until the woman emerged from behind the curtain and gave me the signal to move. From the side of the camera, she pulled out an envelope-looking pouch that contained my photograph. It was sealed on all sides and, rather than handing it to me, she placed it at the end of a long row of unopened envelopes on the table behind her.

Now I understood the mob of people, they were all waiting to have their aura photo interpreted by the radiant woman sitting in the director's chair that I had seen before. I was ushered into the crowd of people waiting in line to meet her. Now having a much better look at her, I watched as she opened photograph after photograph, casually interpreting the colors and patterns she noticed in people's auras. Person after person squealed at the opportunity to have their photo read and snap their selfie with her. I could see why!

She seemed petite, but it's hard to say for certain since she was sitting up in a director's chair. She had short silver hair, cut in a tight little bob. She was probably in her seventies, wore large orange framed glasses, and very minimal jewelry. She had one large ring in the middle of her left hand, with the largest pearl I had ever seen! She wore a red, yellow, green, and blue thick striped muumuu dress, and her bright blue eyes beamed past her giant glasses. She was fabulous and reminded me a lot of an equally fabulous musician I had the pleasure of seeing play piano in Austin. If he had a twin sister, this gal would be it!

Enjoying every second of watching her interpret the photos, I waited patiently for my turn. I watched a young man's eyes pop out of his head in line before me in awe of her, and it warmed my heart to no end. The remaining giggling selfies were had, and it was now my turn. As she said goodbye to the young man before me, she reached for my envelope on the table.

Softly greeting me, she began to peel open my photograph. I was surprisingly giddy. She laid eyes on my photo for the very first time and let out a moan I hadn't heard her make in the time I had been standing by and observing her with others. She looked up at me and then back down to my photo in her hand.

"Mmmm!" she exclaimed, as she looked up at me again. She shook her attention back down to my photo and then spoke. "We'll get back to that in a minute," she said as she turned the photo around to show me. She pointed to the white area above my head and explained that most people have speckles of white around them representing their spirit guides that are with them. "You have a solid band of white around you," she said, "you roll with a posse around you at all times! I hope you know how divinely protected you are?" I felt very comforted at that moment and had this deep knowing inside that I knew what she was saying was the truth.

"Now, back to the good stuff!" she exclaimed. "Do you see this purple hue over you?" She was pointing at my photo. As I nodded, she looked me dead in the eye and the entire convention center fell silent.

"You are a visionary," she explained. "People with this hue of purple are here to make a massive impact in the world. You are going to affect millions of people's lives in this lifetime."

She must have noticed the deer-in-the-headlights gaze on my face and went on to explain, "You, my dear, are going to change the world. You are going to change millions of lives."

I just nodded and blinked, as if my entire life's purpose had just been revealed to me for the very first time. I had no concern to explore the 'how,' I just soaked up every word she spoke to me. Still floating in a silent conference hall, just her and I, she softly grabbed my hand and said, "You have a tribe of guides with you at all times, but you will not have to fulfill this mission alone. You have big work here to do. Please hear my words," she concluded.

I nodded and took a deep breath for the first time in what seemed like a long time. She squeezed my hand and smiled radiantly at me, her baby blues piercing mine through her giant orange glasses. I thanked her graciously and asked the gal behind me to capture a photograph for me.

I remember my friend saying I looked like I had just seen a ghost, as I fumbled through a goodbye and began making my way back through the convention center towards the sunlight. There are very few moments in my life that I remember in such detail that I can still feel them in my bones, and that exchange was one of them. As I made my way back to my car, through the sea of guests and merchants, the world was still silent. There was no fear, there was no anxiety, I was merely digesting the news I had just received with a feeling of absolute certainty that I somehow deep inside of me already knew that she was right. My life would never be the same.

Arriving back to Huntington Beach, still in a bit of a fog from my experience, I pulled out my collection of oracle cards and sat down at my dining room table. I know that whenever I need additional guidance, there will always be a deck that jumps out at me to use that day. I pulled out a deck called "Earth Power Oracle: an atlas for the soul" by Stacey DeMarco. It was the first time that I had felt intuitively guided to use this deck.

I opened the box, and as I began shuffling the cards, I whispered, "God, Angels, Universe, Spirit Guides of the highest truth and compassion, please show me what else I need to know today." One card fell out of the deck and onto the table.

It was "The Tarkine," and the card read, "Growth is good, but I acknowledge it can sometimes be painful. I accept my wild soul. I can be alone and connected." Behind these words was an illustration of a golden forest surrounding a foggy river, and a lone creature sitting at the edge of the water. The animal looked like a combination of a small bear and a kangaroo; I did not recognize it any more specifically.

Still carrying a similar sense of calm as I had felt having my aura photo interpreted, I opened the oracle guidebook to read more about this card. The writeup explained the key energies of the card were growth, wilderness, secrets, and isolation. There were GPS coordinates to a location in Tasmania, Australia. The primary elements at play were earth and water. There was a lovely description of De-Marco's experience sitting on the edge of the water, meeting her first of many wombats, taking in the biodiverse lands of the Aboriginal peoples who made their homes there for thousands of years. The section was concluded with "When you visit" guidelines and suggestions that made it so very clear the decision was already made that I was going.

I pulled out my laptop, entered in the noted GPS coordinates, and began to explore the deep history of the Tarkine. Within an hour I had found a guide I trusted and was coordinating travel plans to Australia. Without question, I booked a flight to Melbourne, a swanky hotel on the river to explore the city for a few days, a puddle jumper to Tasmania, and a six-night backpacking excursion through the Tarkine Rainforest. I had no idea what I was getting myself into, but I was getting myself into it.

27

The Tarkine

Arriving on the last flight into Tasmania, I was one of seven people in the entire airport, along with one last security guard in a dark abandoned taxi waiting zone. As the airport doors clicked locked behind me, I felt an immediate sense of panic as the lone security guard strolled toward us. "You all waiting for a taxi?" he inquired. The six other travelers and I silently nodded, as we saw approximately zero taxis in sight.

The guard pulled out his phone and began chatting with an operator. There was one taxi running and he was on his way back for the first pickup. I was fourth in line. The panic started to set in when I realized that this was going to be a very long night. Already approaching midnight, I knew my 5:00 a.m. pickup was going to arrive far too quickly.

My social anxiety of being trapped without a bathroom kicked in as the taxi returned forty minutes later for the second pickup. Even in the brisk clear air of the night, my body began to sweat in all the uncomfortable places. I took off my bag and sat down on the curb against my pack. Completely helpless to hasten my arrival to my motel, I settled into my seat, thanking God that I was at least in a country where I could comfortably speak the language.

By the grace of God, another taxi came around and I was safely delivered to my motel an hour and forty-five minutes later. With only a couple of hours left for some shuteye, I got on top of the blankets of my bed and laid there with all my clothes on. I laid there with absolute certainty that my room was haunted and very dirty. I prayed to whoever would listen to help me get through the night and protect me while I slept.

After what felt like half an hour later, I rolled out of bed to turn off my alarm. Then I fumbled my way into the bathroom to have a good scrub before being off the grid for the next week. Fully covered in soap, I reached up to adjust the showerhead to rinse my tiny body. As I loosely gripped the edges of the showerhead it came crashing to the floor, shattering the temperature gauge on its way down. Fully pressurized water was now spraying directly into my face!

Attempting to reattach the showerhead, I only successfully sprayed water over the entire bathroom floor. The rubber connector had snapped, and the connection was now impossible to reattach. Not trying to flood the entire room, I dropped the showerhead and redirected my attention to the temperature gauge. With a firehose spraying me in my face, and nowhere else to turn in the tiny shower, I dug my fingernails into the crevices of the broken knob.

Slowly turning it a millimeter at a time, I was finally able to get the water completely turned off. I was still uncomfortably covered in soap when I heard a car honking outside and began to fully panic. I managed to wrap myself in a wet towel to answer the knock at my door. There stood my bright-eyed guides and a van full of smiling faces. The look on my face must have painted enough of a picture for them as I breathlessly explained the situation and asked for two more minutes to throw my clothes on. Using the dripping towel to wipe the excess soap off my body, I scrambled to write a note to the hotel staff apologizing for the incident in the bathroom. Still damp, I grabbed my pack and my boots and joined my new pals outside.

What an epic way to start our adventure, they all clamored. Awkwardly agreeing, I handed over my pack and climbed into the van.

We made our way to the edge of the rainforest, and I quickly got to know my adventure mates. There were two guides, Jake and Natalie, an elderly couple, a middle-aged woman, another gal about my age, and a sassy older gentleman whom I instantly knew would be my favorite new companion. Together we were intimately going to explore The Tarkine. By the time we turned off the paved road, I was stoked for the epic adventure ahead. Cruising down a very bumpy dirt road for an uncomfortable amount of time, the van suddenly stopped in the middle of its path. "This is it!" Jake explained excitedly.

How on earth he knew this was the appropriate entrance to the rainforest, I had no idea. It looked like all of the other tree lines we had been driving through for the last few miles, with no pullout or sign that it was time to stop. The path went on before us, but we were parked right there and began unloading.

Natalie took off into the trees while the rest of us began piling up our packs and supplies. Taking turns finding our first "rest stops," we all awkwardly peered around awaiting Natalie's return. Just as I was thoroughly getting confused, a rustling appeared from the trees. Natalie was pulling a cart of sorts that would carry our supplies into the camp. It was a homemade rig that looked like someone had built a rack on top of a handheld pallet jack. Without asking questions, we all helped in loading the cart full of our supplies.

Soon, we were packed and ready to move along. Jake asked if anyone wanted to throw their packs on top of Natalie's rig. The others agreed, creating a wobbly mountain of backpacks on top of the coolers and supplies. Feeling guilty for Natalie to carry the whole load, I opted out. Determined to fully commit to this experience, I naively committed to carrying my backpack into camp, while Natalie and our supply rig took off to the left and Jake guided us all forward into the forest ahead.

By about a mile and a half into our forest ascension, I regretted not surrendering my pack to Natalie's rig. Now sweating my ass off, and clearly out of shape, I tightened up my straps and leaned into the experience. Thank goodness the travel guide booking my excursion had convinced me to rent a walking stick. Had I not, I probably would have been on my hands and knees crawling up that rainforest floor.

Just shy of three miles later, the rainforest floor began to level, and camp began to appear. There was a small wooden shack, with a large wooden platform jetting towards the top canopies of the trees. This was our camp kitchen and dining area. There was a long, gorgeous wood table, and several small counters to prepare our food. As I meandered over to the edge of the deck, taking in the breathtaking expansiveness before me, I heard a familiar rustle of Natalie and her rig. She had taken an alternative route that had been loosely cleared to pull the supply cart into camp.

As Natalie began to set up our kitchen, Jake walked each of us in opposite directions to our tent site. The kitchen compound was the center of our camp, and each of us had a secluded little area off the beaten path. While in my tent, I was far enough away to not see anyone, but close enough to vaguely hear chatter in the distance. This was the most off the grid I had ever been, and I had conveniently omitted the tidbit of information that I had never actually been camping before. I had just been told how divinely protected I was, so I just rolled with it.

The next six days and nights were experiences that could fill entire novels. Each morning, the crew and I met at the community table for instant coffee and the breakfast Natalie had prepared for us. Everything was intentionally planned so that we could experience the local fare of the island, and plant-based meals were prepared out on our day trips. After we finished our cup of joes, we secured our day packs with water bladders and took off into the forest.

Each day we explored a different area of the wilderness, and no two days were alike. The first day, we ventured into a higher ridge, full of grasslands and sunshine. We learned of Jake's favorite game of identifying the dung and met many local snakes living in the brush. I fell in love with the way Jake geeked out at every little thing he had to share with us. He was young, only twenty-four, and clearly aligned with his life's true purpose. He was the best guide one could ever hope to have in the middle of a rainforest, on an island, in the middle of the ocean. That would be the last day we would see direct sunlight.

Each following day after that, we ventured deeper into the rainforest only by the ambient light glowing amongst the trees. Every turn we took was fascinating and magical, and there was not a moment of downtime when I was not in complete awe and wonder of this sacred land. The forest was rich with energy and thriving with the history of its evolution and past. We saw where fires had blazed through, but never burned to destruction. We saw fingerprints of lightning strikes and overturned root systems the size of houses.

There were two things in particular that I found most fascinating about this sacred land: there were very few bugs, and the forest floor was not solid. The Tarkine is one of the rarest rainforests in the world. The average age of trees in the forest surpasses six hundred years old. This rainforest is so old that it predates pollinating plants. Where there are no pollinating plants, there are no bugs. Where there are no bugs, there aren't many birds. A majority of the wildlife in the Tarkine are listed as endangered or rare. So rare that we were told how blessed we would be to come across the Tasmanian Devil responsible for the droppings we had been following.

The other pleasant surprise of these full-day excursions was how comfortable the hikes were to my feet. The forest floor was alive with buoyancy. The lands were so undisturbed that there wasn't even enough activity to pack down the layers of fallen leaves and branches that made up the forest floor. It was as if we were walking along the tops of millions of layers of bark and leaves. It wasn't like snow or clouds we could fall through; it was just soft and forgiving with each, and every step. The entire ecosystem of the rainforest was below the ground. Millions of species of fungi ruled this sacred land. There was not much wildlife that could be seen with my naked eye, but Jake assured me that it was thriving and well beneath our feet.

We explored and swam in the river, and we meditated inside the hollow hole of a tree that towered above my line of sight. Every moment of that trip far surpassed my wildest expectations. With each passing day, I became more connected to the land and comfortable in the silence of her majesty. I had never felt so a part of and whole, connected to nothing and everything.

I can describe the lessons that came through my time in the Tarkine in one experience. One evening, midweek, we had returned to camp as the dusk melted the light into the trees. I sat, quietly in contemplation, staring off the edge of the deck when one of my new mates told me that I was up next for the opportunity to take a shower. Unsure that I would be given the opportunity, I reveled in the excitement to explore the bathing situation Natalie and Jake had created.

I followed the suggested path down into a canyon where I was at once stopped in my tracks. I was startled and breathless. There before my eyes was a disc-shaped fungus growing out of the side of the canyon wall. It bulged out before me in the most fluorescent orange I had ever seen. No highlighter I had ever owned compared to the orange of this mushroom. I basked in its delicate beauty as the light slowly continued to melt from the rainforest around me.

Then I looked up and saw a small hut just past the beaming mushroom. It was as if she was guarding the gates to the water, it was magnificent. As I arrived at the hut, I found a wooden bucket the size of a large mixing bowl, one coffee cup, and two small bottles containing eco-approved soap and shampoo. There was a note that said please fill the bucket one time with water and enjoy only the selected soaps we have provided.

Gingerly turning the knob, in order not to create another shower fiasco, I began to fill my bucket with water. As it reached the top, I turned off the faucet and scooted the bucket aside. Then I grabbed the plastic coffee cup and dunked it in the water. To my surprise, it only took two coffee cups of water to completely wet my body. As I lathered myself with the soap provided, I peered out from the shower hut which was sitting on a small platform at the edge of the cliff, completely overlooking the entire forest below me.

As I lathered my hair, my heart began to sink into the divine simplicity of the moment. I was naked, on the edge of this cliff, in the middle of the most incredible land I had ever seen, and it only took one bucket of water to completely cleanse my body. Coffee cup in hand as I rinsed myself clean, tears began to stream down my face as I watched the last moments of light dance from the trees.

As I realized that I still had half a bucket of water left beside me, I silently wept at the depth of the connection I had to Mother Earth at that moment. How wasteful I had felt for the water consumption I had used washing my hair every day back home. How wasteful I had been, allowing the water to run while it tempered to my preferred scalding degrees.

I wept in gratitude for her lessons that I am but a visitor here to her sacred lands on Earth. I am but a guest causing a path of destruction to her divinity and creation. I am but a spec of existence in the grand scheme of her majesty. As the salty tears blended into the water dripping from my body, I picked up the wooden bucket of my remaining water. Setting it on the ledge of the hut, I thanked her for this experience and offered the water back to her as a gesture of my gratitude. As the remaining water poured out of my bucket, a calm came over me that she appreciated and forgave me. I knew that now that I knew better, I could do better.

28

A New Relationship with my Higher Power

Just a few months after connecting with the land in the Tarkine, I had a deep calling to attend a Reiki certification program at a beautiful meditation studio in Los Angeles. As divine timing would have it, an emergency came up, causing me to reschedule my Reiki Level 1 experience at the very last minute. The studio graciously accepted my needs and offered me a combined Reiki 1 + 2 immersion experience the following month. I was guided to my Reiki Master, and yet again my understanding of a Higher Power began to change.

I had just been Reiki attuned for the very first time and was released into creative expression when I grabbed a golden yellow marker, and my hand began interpreting the experience that was still occurring in my mind's eye. On the paper before me emerged a golden energy field, a vertical oval shape, representing a body, not solidly formed, but representing a pulsating of condensed energy from the core of the oval. A circle appeared at the top of the oval. This circle appeared as more of swirling golden energy. This circle of swirling energy then had an energy field radiating outwardly from it. Above the swirling golden circle was a bright bluish-white funnel of energy pouring infinitely into it from the heavens.

Just as the image appeared before me, my body settled with a deep sense of contentment that I had just witnessed, as if from out of my body, the integration of this divine energy from the universal source into my soul. We were now entangled and connected, and from the very first second this energy penetrated my earthly being, I knew I had met a familiar home. It was as if a divine remembering had been cracked open from behind a barricaded cave. This energy felt familiar, and I knew that it was safe to receive.

After completing my golden energy reflection, I picked up a faint white marker and began to trace the edges of the paper with the words now pouring out of me:

"With each wave of energy, the Gold energy rocked back and forth from the top. As more Reiki was received the Gold became more centered until it was still. Then the Gold was taken over by pure white light. All Gold was gone and all that was left was the pure white light. Calm, pure, powerful, beautiful. It is this purest energy that will heal each of us. It is Source. She is in me. She has invited me to spread this light to all who are willing to receive her light + love."

Reiki is a sacred Japanese healing art that literally translates into Divine Universal Life Force Energy. (Pronounced Ray-Key) Reiki is a healing modality that is available to everyone to raise their vibrations for a life of maximum joy and empowerment. Practicing and/or receiving Reiki is taking the initiative to dissolve your ego and realign with your highest self.

Everything and everyone has a living energy field, commonly referred to as our aura. Reiki works within that energy field to balance it and return it to a natural state of homeostasis. The electrical and magnetic qualities of Reiki can even be scientifically measured.

Bernadette Doran, BS, RMT, explains in her 2009 publication, *The Science Behind Reiki*, "One of the most basic laws of physics, Ampere's Law, explains the electrical and magnetic energies in and around the human body. Ampere's Law says that when electrical currents flow through conductors, whether they are wires or living tissue, a magnetic field is produced in the surrounding space. Since living tissue – including the heart and other muscles, the brain, and other organs – conducts electricity, the laws of physics mean they create a magnetic field around the body, called the bio magnetic field."

Similar to other commonly used sophisticated tools of Western medicine, pulsing magnetic fields can jumpstart the healing of tissue, bone, and other body parts. Dr. John Zimmerman measured the magnetic field frequencies of Reiki practitioners while they worked on clients and found that they all emitted similar frequencies from their hands.

Reiki Practitioners are not giving away any of their energy to the recipients, rather they are acting as the conduit for the frequency of the Universal Life Force Energy to flow through. Doran explains, "Some scientists call it the "tuning fork" of the planet, claiming that it generates natural healing properties when living things are entrained to its rhythm."

Being one who loves to geek out on the scientific reasoning behind any spiritual practice, there have been many discoveries supporting the use of Reiki healing. Very prestigious medical institutions, such as Johns Hopkins and the Mayo Clinic are now even integrating Reiki into their hospitals.

According to the Center for Integrative Medicine at Cleveland Clinic, "Reiki complements all other types of medical and therapeutic treatments. Reiki treatment should not be used as a substitute for consultation of a physician, a practitioner of natural therapeutics, or a psychotherapist. Reiki can increase the efficacy of other types of healing."

Reiki treatment may support the following:

- bring about a peaceful, deep state of relaxation
- dissolve energy blockages and tension
- detoxify the body
- support the well-being of a person receiving traditional medical treatments that are debilitating (e.g., chemotherapy, radiation, surgery, kidney dialysis)
- supply universal life force energy to the body
- stimulate the body's immune system
- help to relieve pain
- stimulate tissue and bone healing after injury or surgery
- increase the vibrational frequency on physical, mental, emotional, and spiritual levels

Reiki has emerged more so now than ever before, during a time of deep awakening on our planet. Now that we are understanding the physical effects of our emotions and the energy in our bodies and overall wellbeing, Reiki is an extremely gentle and effective way to reconnect with ourselves - mind, body + spirit - to release what is no longer serving us. Reiki is delivered with the intention that it is always for whatever is of our highest good.

While I originally had intended to dive deeper into Reiki healing for personal use, after years of receiving treatment from a Reiki Master in Arizona, I had found myself being given the opportunity to now become certified as a Reiki Practitioner. Not only did this attune me to be able to deliver Reiki to others, but I also became proficient in distance healing.

The beautiful thing about Reiki is that being Source energy, or Universal Life Force Energy, we are working at higher frequencies than that of modern technologies. The energy cannot be disturbed by time or space, thus Practitioners attuned to Level 2 can deliver Reiki to anyone on the planet. Even more incredible, since Reiki is not limited to time or space, we can also deliver Reiki to the past and present.

It is common after receiving this level of attunement to participate in a self-healing journey delivering Reiki to one's past lives, at conception, at birth, at one year old, at two years old, etc. until reaching the present day. Reiki can also be delivered to an event or a time in the future. Whether launching an event or special project or penetrating every word that you are now reading, Reiki healing can be transmitted to anything or anyone. Other common uses of Reiki include blessing our food, healing our pets, clearing stagnant energies in physical spaces, and releasing energetic cords and ties with others.

The possibilities really are truly endless, but there are two instances where I have found distance Reiki to be truly invaluable: with burn victims and with those who have experienced sexual assault or physical trauma. Attunement to Distance Reiki allows a practitioner to deliver energy healing to individuals for whom physical touch may not be possible or appropriate. In my humble opinion, deep soul healing cannot be forced. One must feel emotionally and energetically safe within the depths of their nervous system to bring about any willingness for healing and growth. In cases such as these, Reiki can provide an opportunity to begin healing gently and subtly.

Reiki healing resonates with me in a way that Western medicine never could. I am not the type of person who is interested in a pill or a Band-Aid for my problems. Coming from decades of numbing and substance abuse, I am much more interested in an integrative and holistic approach that is going to allow me to address the root cause of the issue. When I know better, I can do better and when we heal ourselves, we heal the world.

29

You Don't Need a Guru

For the year or so after my Practitioner Level Reiki attunement, I began developing Distance Reiki as my business. I began by offering months and months of energetic exchange sessions, no-cost sessions in exchange for testimonials, and began to hone my confidence for my practice. I was receiving incredible feedback and really loving the work I was able to do to help others.

Then the world was hit with a global pandemic and my Reiki Master Practitioner certification was postponed. As divine timing would have it, however, the originally scheduled date fell right in the middle of my time back home as my father passed. I wouldn't have been able to make it live in California anyhow. As the world began to migrate into completely digital models of business, the Reiki world was already well equipped. We had already been trained to practice and deliver Reiki remotely, so this transition was seamless and a breeze.

After a few attempts to reschedule, my cohort of Reiki pals and our Reiki Master agreed on an early summer date and made the decision that we were not going to let this pandemic dictate our purpose. Our services were needed more than ever, and we all agreed to meet virtually to continue along our path. I planned my departure from Arizona immediately following the completion of my Level Three Master Practitioner certification and boy am I glad that I did.

My experience in Levels One and Two was all about activating this beautiful connection with the higher cosmos and beginning to explore breaking the molds of traditional healing and awareness. It lovingly cracked me open to the spiritual possibilities and kickstarted my journey to self-discovery. If my Level Two attunement was a pillowy landing in the gymnastics foam pit, my Level Three attunement was being dropped out of a skyscraper water slide in Las Vegas. You know the ones where the floor completely drops out beneath you, and you're plummeted down the shoot, lose your bikini top, and get a whole bunch of water up your butt? That is how I would describe the integration of my Master Practitioner attunement.

The actual attunement and training were incredible, gorgeous, and insanely powerful, but this was the point in the journey where shit got really real. We received the Master symbols and wildly next-level tools and meditations, and the work we could now do as Practitioners was quite miraculous. However, the spiritual process of becoming Reiki attuned is not only about what we can do for others. In fact, you don't have to work with others to go through the attunement process. It is in and of itself a deeply spiritual personal development experience. The process from Level One attunement to Reiki Master is all about our own personal journey back to our highest self. Should you choose to actively practice as a business is completely, and solely up to everyone's path.

On a personal level, Level Three is all about the shadow work we each have to do in this lifetime. I believe that we each arrive here with a set of lessons and patterns to process and heal in this lifetime. We all have a different set of karmic experiences we are given to experience, and no two people's experiences are the same. Our curriculum for this lifetime is determined by our previous experiences and how we are here to learn and grow in this evolution of the human experience. While we all have individual curriculums, we are all in this universal schoolhouse called Earth.

We receive the teachers and the relationships that we need along the way, but no one else can do this work for us. It is solely our responsibility to do the work. We can consciously or subconsciously choose not to do the work and continue our lives on the hamster wheel of what others have determined we should be doing, or we can break free from that matrix to fulfill our purpose and our path, and not repeat this experience the next go around.

Every single experience that we have is guiding us back to our higher self and our purpose here in this lifetime. Every hurt, every success, every heartbreak, every jaw-dropping joy is a mirror reflecting the parts of ourselves that we need at that moment. As the late Ram Dass has famously said, "We're all just walking each other home."

As we all have masculine and feminine energies within us, we each also have light and darkness. The light is the version of ourselves that we share consciously with the world and our shadow is the part of our personality that our ego unconsciously attempts to keep from existence. Just because we cannot always see our shadow does not mean that it does not exist. When I speak about shadow work, or "doing the work," I am referring to the active process of bringing the unconscious darkness into the light. The shadow is not bad, evil, or dangerous. I believe it is the roadmap of the deepest work we are here to process in this lifetime. As Psychologist Carl Jung has said, "Until you make the unconscious conscious, it will direct your life and you will call it fate."

In *The Philosophical Tree (1945)*, Jung writes:

"Filling the conscious mind with ideal conceptions is a characteristic of Western theosophy, but not the confrontation with the shadow and the world of darkness. One does not become enlightened by imagining figures of light, but by making the darkness conscious."

"A man who is unconscious of himself acts in a blind, instinctive way and is in addition fooled by all the illusions that arise when he sees everything that he is not conscious of in himself coming to meet him from outside as projections upon his neighbor."

Each experience that we have in this lifetime is merely a mirror being held up, reflecting the projections of what we are here to process. Our shadow reflects us in ways we may call fate, what triggers us, what harms us, and what continues to cycle through as patterned behaviors and experiences. The fastest and easiest way to check-in with our shadow is to examine our intimate relationships.

If shadow work is new to you, I encourage you to look at the patterns of your past relationships. Are you constantly attracting the same partner over and over? Are you experiencing the same trauma or heartbreak over and over? This pattern is an indication of work that needs to be done. This can only be achieved by each individual when they become willing to do the work. Until then, we continue informing the universe to please give us more of the same experiences until we are willing to open our eyes to see the truth.

If the concept of shadow work is triggering or terrifying to you, this is a message that says your soul is ready to continue this work. We are triggered most by the work we are now ready to do within ourselves. At this point in the book, if the words I am lovingly delivering to you are triggering, I am thrilled for you! That tells me that you are approaching the point of willingness. I love you and honor you as you begin to see yourself in the mirror. It is a safe space here, but you must be willing, and it takes what it takes to arrive at willingness. You will continue to be guided to your shadow until you are ready to get off the hamster wheel. While it may seem scary every time, trust me when I say the peace and serenity that comes along with this work is well worth the price of admission.

If you are in the phase of spiritual work or personal development that I like to call addicted to collecting tools, where you continue to jump from one self-help book to the next, or from one coaching program after another, please take a deep breath and hear what I am about to say:

You do not need another guru. The guru is already inside of you. You already know the path; it is your job now to stop collecting other people's tools and actually *do the work*.

If this stings to hear or leaves you flabbergasted that I could call you out in such a way, then this is your message: it is time to break the patterns. The buck stops here. You have all that you need at this moment, and it is time. Go forth and shine, my friend! *It is time to do the work!* This is the unraveling. This is the work of peace. This is a great remembering. Whatever you want to call it, this is the work!

30

Please Be Kind to My Friend

Having a deep certainty that I could never go back to my old life and its toxic experiences; it became apparent that I had no idea who I was inside. My sponsor loves to explain it this way: that I am peeling back one more layer of my onion with each discovery and experience. While I appreciate the analogy, I feel more like an onion that has spent decades adding on more sweaters to try to fit into these molds that I held in such high regard.

I felt like I had painfully peeled off the last sweater and with it came the first few rotted layers of my onion, like a partially healed scab that gets stuck in the stickiest parts of a Band-Aid. It all felt so painful and raw. I felt vulnerable and confused, and often like I was crawling in my skin, never knowing what the fuck to do with my hands.

I felt like a brand-new baby giraffe trying to figure out how to stand on my wobbly legs for the very first time. I had to learn who I was, not the version that everyone on the outside had seen, but that tiny little light inside me - who was she? I have always been taught that the rooms of my 12-Step program are my safest place to splat my shit, and as I began to share more about my experiences, three interesting things began to happen.

When I began to share about this scary, raw, "I don't know what to do with my hands" experience, other people in the meetings would nod their heads and laugh. Women would validate my feelings, share their versions of this experience and how temporary it all was in the grand scheme of my recovery. They would remind me to take it all one day at a time, and to please be kind to myself.

The second perplexing thing that kept happening was that people kept asking me what I did for self-care. Self-care, really?! That felt like a fluffy extravagance that was so far from my ability at that time. When asked, I would brush the question off with some version of, "Oh, you know, the normal stuff" and then awkwardly try to change the subject.

The third thing was a memory. I kept having a memory of the conversation that I had with the husband of one of my best friends. He was also in the program and after a meeting one night we got to chatting. He asked me where I was in my step work and was deeply concerned when I told him what I was sitting on. He removed the cigar from his mouth, looked me square in the eyes, and said, "I am terrified for you."

This one little conversation struck a chord so deep within me that I immediately finished what had taken me years to fumble through. In one month I had worked through more of my step work than I had in years.

For whatever reason, I heard him that night in a way that I deeply needed to hear. As I continued to share about my new rawness, the memory of that conversation kept surfacing in my mind. Willing to learn who this version of me was, I prayed for the next indicated step and for clarity on what I was not seeing. After the third or fourth time remembering the conversation about how terrified my friend was, it all clicked - I still had some amends to make.

I notified my sponsor of my new realization and she had me pull out the next card. My remaining amends were written on neon-colored notecards, in a worn-out plastic baggie that lived permanently in the bottom of my backpack. It was time to pull it out and give the cards a shuffle. I left it up to my Higher Power to determine who was next, and I got to work.

As I moved through some powerful experiences of making amends, I continued sharing about my new rawness in my meetings. Others continued to share their experience, strength, and hope and continued encouraging me to please be kind to myself. I still didn't understand all this talk about being kind to myself, so I kept praying for the next indicated step and for clarity on what I was not seeing.

Turns out self-care is not just about bubble baths and mani-pedis. Sure, that can be part of your routine, if that's your cup of tea, but I have come to learn that self-care is about being kind to yourself, overall. People kept telling me, "Please be kind to yourself," or "Please be kind to my friend" and I would roll my eyes inside having no idea what they were even talking about.

But being kind to yourself *is* self-care! Unfortunately, there is no rule book for self-care, but there are a shit ton of free resources on the inter-webs, and I have come to learn that self-care is a deeply personal and customizable experience, and there is no right or wrong way to do it. For me, I can break down my ideas of self-care into a few simple buckets:

- Pampering
- Mental Health
- Physical Health
- Spiritual Health
- The Fuck It Bucket

Pampering:

In the pampering bucket, I have two categories: routine pampering and luxurious pampering. In the routine pampering category I place activities like bubble baths, getting my hair done, at-home face masks, and lunch dates with friends. These are things that I do regularly, but not every day. They are special treats that I allow myself to participate in just because they bring me joy. I do not put conditions on them, such as I must complete this work thing in order to use the special bath bombs. I allow myself to do things that bring me joy, fit comfortably in my current budget, and are just acts of love to *me*.

The second category, luxurious pampering, is for things that may require more time or money. These items may be special treats that are contingent on achieving a particular milestone, or that happens less frequently than the routine pampering. For me, luxurious pampering activities include taking a road trip, getting a massage, reorganizing my closet, cooking a big family meal for all my friends, or going to the beach in the middle of a "workday."

The most important thing to note about pampering as self-care is that it must bring you joy. Doing things that you feel guilty about doing is not self-care. Chances are that you will self-sabotage later, in some other way, if you pamper yourself in a way that makes you feel guilty. This leads me to the second most important point about pampering, it doesn't have to cost a lot of money. I firmly believe that there are pampering self-care activities for every kind of expression of love.

I grew up in a household that loved hosting holidays and dinners and was incapable of cooking any small amount of food. For me, I receive great joy in cooking for others. There is a special kind of love that is shared in spending time, getting my hands dirty in the kitchen, dancing around while preparing a meal for myself and others. If I am stressed out, or really in my head, one of my go-to self-care moves is to get my ass in the kitchen. Food prepared with love nourishes the soul in a way that can be felt and tasted. Just ask anyone that ever ate one of my dad's pizzas!

Mental Health:

The mental health bucket is extremely important to me. Being someone who has spent many years battling anxiety, depression, and substance abuse, I have done and put a lot of research and experimentation into this self-care bucket. I feel like I could write an entire book on just mental health self-care, and who knows, maybe that will be book number two. For me, I can break this bucket into:

- How I speak to myself
- What I consume
- How I recharge

At first, I didn't believe how powerful my thoughts and words could be until I really started to examine the causes and conditions of my mental health. Whether we call them the voices in our head, the angel and devil on our shoulder, or the sound of our mother pouring through us, we are all directly affected by the thoughts we choose to think and the words we choose to speak. When left to their own devices, the shitty committee in my head can be real assholes!

The voices in my head default to topics of guilt, shame, and remorse. I could justify all the reasons why I was undeserving, not good enough, and unlovable at the drop of a hat but was deeply uncomfortable accepting even a simple compliment. How we think and speak about ourselves gives everyone else in the universe permission to treat us that way as well. When we begin to examine how we speak to ourselves, if done honestly, we can illuminate many areas of opportunity for growth.

One of the simplest ways to reprogram how we speak to ourselves is through 'I AM' affirmations. An affirmation is a mantra or incantation that one repeats until the statement becomes a belief. The key to affirmations is consistency in repetition and having the willingness in your body to change old thoughts. You can say "I am happy. I am happy. I am happy." all you want, but if you are resistant to the belief that you can change and be happy, the result will be much slower to appear. I love to say that we only need to crack open the door of willingness for miracles to come barging through.

Sample 'I AM' affirmations for beginners:

- I am beautiful
- I am enough
- I am worthy of love
- I am kind + patient
- I am divinely protected
- I am divinely guided

Samples of more advanced affirmations:

- Abundance flows freely to me in expected + unexpected ways
- It is easy for me to receive _____ in safe + easy ways
- My work is of high service + my clients see incredible results
- As I continue to love myself, I inspire others all around me to do the same
- The more fun I have, the more money I make
- I accept and love myself wholly and completely

To amplify the effects of affirmations, practice saying them to yourself in the mirror. This can be deeply uncomfortable at first, but I promise you the more you can look yourself in the eye, the more freely self-care of all forms will flow for you. One fun little trick that one of my besties and I practice together is to respond with, "Thank you, it's true!" whenever we receive a compliment. You will be surprised how challenging it can be at first. Now, however, we embrace our compliments and constantly rope others around us into our little game. Our circle is growing quite proficient in the department of accepting compliments!

Beyond just the thoughts we think, and affirmations we speak to ourselves, it is gravely important to examine the words we speak in our daily lives. Reframing the words we use is a habit that takes practice, but it is very doable once you begin to have the willingness to speak with kinder words. For example, if you are someone that easily gets agitated and responds with comments like, "That sucks," "That isn't fair," "That figures," "This always happens to me," try considering "Isn't that interesting?" This is my favorite reframe for anything that makes me angry, pissed off, annoyed, or frustrated.

"Isn't that interesting?" allows me to simply observe the situation at hand, rather than allowing my entire emotional response to be activated into a spiral of self-pity or victimization. Simply observing gives me that brief moment of pause to decide if I am willing to allow the experience to receive the first gut reaction. Oftentimes the answer is no - that situation is not worth the initial reaction I was going to give it. So practicing the reframed response to be "Isn't that interesting?" alleviates a lot of unnecessary stress and anger!

Another observation to notice is the words we immediately choose when we feel discomfort in our body. If you have a headache, do you jump to, "I have a brain tumor and I'm dying"? If you are suddenly feeling moody, do you immediately say, "I need a coffee," or "I can never catch a break"? Instead, pause and check in with your body to see what it is trying to tell you.

One great slogan to incorporate is H.A.L.T. which means asking yourself these questions, "am I Hungry, Angry, Lonely, or Tired?" It is so easy to jump to conclusions about all the external reasons that we suddenly feel a certain way, but nine times out of ten we are probably just hungry, angry, lonely, or tired, or often a combination of a few! Beginning to check in with my body, rather than just respond with conditioned words has been massively powerful in transforming my mental health.

Next in the Mental Health bucket is what I consume. We currently live in a world that is overstimulated and oversaturated. Humans are addicted to screens, scrolling, and sharing. We have transitioned into an age ruled by social media and consumerism. Our apps learn and advance in ways that allow their algorithms to show us and sell us what corporations want us to consume.

If this is the first time anyone has told you that we are being brainwashed, congratulations and welcome! If you haven't heard this before, or are not sure, let me ask you one simple question - have you ever talked about something, or researched something, and then started receiving ads on social media about that very thing? Everything we do on our miracle devices is linked, tracked, and used to sell us something.

Of course, there are two sides to every coin, I will be the first to admit that my business and the success of many other artists and entrepreneurs are highly supported by social media. I also love the ability to stay connected with friends and family all over the world. It's a double-edged sword, and with all things, I believe it is all about intention and awareness.

About eight years ago, I was an avid weight trainer and I hated everything about corporate gyms and the overall energy around the fitness industry. It was heavily designed to tell you what was wrong with you and then sell you a solution to fix your problem, be it personal training or some workout program. I hated how damaging it was in its harmful marketing and sales tactics that I was hell-bent on leaving my career in success coaching to become a personal trainer and open a brick + mortar facility that was all about empowerment and positive body healing.

I drafted business plans and buried myself in my certification education. As I was nearing the end of my certification training, I noticed an interesting development in the industry. Social media was blowing up with "fitness influencers" with perfectly curated photos and feeds, selling one size fits all fitness programs. You could buy into these programs with promises to look like this person or that person, and these fitness influencers were making bank!

There was one woman in particular who was very popular around this time who specialized in "build your booty" type programs and paraded herself around with a popular supplement company and was marketing herself as the Queen of Booty Building. I am a huge supporter of women making it big in male-dominated industries, and this woman was definitely gorgeous, but it later came out that she had butt implants and had built her millions on the perfectly curated story of being all-natural and having built her butt with the very programs she was selling to millions of us.

This is just one example of how simple it is to create a perfectly curated image on social media that is used to market and sell completely out of integrity and authenticity. This craze of "fitness influencers" blew up like an uncontrolled California wildfire, and it was painful and disgusting to watch. Of course, some people did see great results and not all the work was slimy and misleading, but overall this industry initiated the era of acceptance that creating this social media lifestyle of perfection and glam was normal and realistic.

It was not until very recently that a lot of these millionaire fitness influencers have started to speak out about the harm and danger of portraying this perfect social media life when it was not always authentic. Many now share about their detrimental mental health, eating disorders, and substance abuse - much of which makes it easy to maintain a slender figure with washboard abs.

This was the point in my life where it became incredibly clear to me that it was more important to work with people before they reached the point of being desperate to hire a beautiful model on social media to give them health and nutrition advice. Since then I have also deeply explored the impact of what media I consume and its correlation to my mental health.

The first suggestion that I highly recommend is doing a major overhaul of who you follow on social media. I chose to unfollow any person, brand, or product based on my feelings toward the following questions:

- Is their underlying energy empowering me or tearing me down?
- Is their messaging driven by instigating fear?
- Are they painting an authentic complete picture? (i.e. are they also sharing about the struggles and not so pretty behind the scenes negative results or side effects)
- Are they clear that they are affiliates or brand ambassadors to the brands they promote?
- Are they using their platform to share uncomfortable conversations, or just sell a manicured lifestyle?
- Are they taking part in raising the vibration of the planet?
- Are they participating in the circulation of fear-based media?

These are the types of questions that I ask myself based on my own perspectives, beliefs, and opinions. I strongly encourage you to think about which messages you choose to consume, and if it doesn't fit in those categories, unfollow.

I mentioned awareness and intention, and if this is the first time you are doing a consumption review of your life, please know that this is a process. Now that we are having this conversation, you are gaining awareness and can begin to notice what you are consuming. Once we have the awareness, what we do next becomes a choice. If none of this resonates with you right now, that is okay, you may not be ready yet.

Another important factor in the "what I consume" category is paying attention to my screen time and blue light consumption. The light emulating from our device screens deeply impacts our bodies and our sleep. I have a setting on my phone and laptop to go into the night view before dusk every day. Most modern devices have some version of this setting, and its intention is to reduce the blue light emitted and soften its intensity to a warmer, duller light.

I have noticed a significant difference in my sleep when I am intentional about my screen time before bed. My phone goes into Do Not Disturb every evening 45 minutes before my bedtime so that I am not receiving any notifications or mindlessly scrolling before bed. I also charge my phone across the room, so I am not tempted to pick it up and lay in bed in the morning. I am very intentional about my night and morning consumption because I have noticed a night and day difference in my mental health when I spend more time away from technology and media (both mass media and social media).

For even more advanced practice, try a social media or tech detox for a couple of days. Better yet, start with 24 hours, just for the awareness of how often you default to picking up your devices when you are uncomfortable, bored, alone, stressed, or tired. I'd love to hear your results!

Other ways I am intentional about what I consume include:

- The type of music I listen to
- The conversations I am willing to engage in
- The people I allow into my intimate space
- How I hear about world events
- Where I shop
- What I eat

Lastly, in my mental health bucket is how I recharge. This is deeply personal to everyone, and my way is in no way the proper solution for everyone. How you need to recharge depends on your personality and how you interact with the world. (I also highly recommend learning about your Human Design profile or Astrological Natal Chart to support this bucket)

Astrologically speaking, I am a Gemini Sun, Virgo Rising, Aries Moon. In Human Design I am a pure manifestor with a 2/4 profile. The cliff notes version of what that means for my mental health and recharging is that I present very bubbly and personable but am very introverted inside and prefer to be a hermit in my own little world. I am very selective about the people I choose to be around and often feel energetically, emotionally, and physically drained after being around groups of people.

For me, I need to retreat and recluse in order to recharge. I need to have my own space, and often feel the calmest when traveling or driving in my car alone. I do not have an endless supply of energy like the majority of the world, so when I am tapped, I must recharge, or I produce a deep rage and anger inside. I have learned this lesson on more than one occasion and have studied it intimately with spiritual coaches in great detail.

If I am not in a situation where it is appropriate to get out of the city, have extended time alone, or go for a long drive, then I can practice a few techniques that I can use in a pinch. Showering, swimming, and breathwork are my go-to mini recharge solutions. When I get into the shower, I imagine all of the chaos and noise of the outside world melting off of me and pouring down the drain. I imagine the water is purifying me and removing any energy that is no longer of my highest good.

Swimming in the ocean is one of the most cleansing and grounding activities I can do for myself. The saltwater, energy charged by the moon, the life force energy, is just magical. If you do not have easy access to the beach, any body of water will do. Fresh or saltwater is always preferred to chlorinated swimming pools, but if the intention is there use whatever body of water that you have access to. When I dive into the water, I allow all other energies to be released and cleansed from my body. I surrender to the pulse and the energy of her movements and I just float. To me, being in the ocean is the fastest and most effective way to get right sized and recharged.

Breathwork is another incredible exercise to change my physiology and ground my energy back into my body. When it gets "too peopley out there," as I like to say, I can be anywhere and connect back with my body in this way. There are many intentional combinations and styles of breathwork, but the main premise is to allow your breath to release any energy no longer of your highest good and regain homeostasis back in your body.

For the most basic practice, place one hand on your chest and one hand on your belly. Allow your body to settle and take a deep breath in through your nose, hold at the top, and slowly release from your mouth. It is important to notice if your inhale is stopping in your chest or progressing to your belly. It is so very common that we think a full breath consists of filling our chest and releasing. That is considered a very shallow breath, and a full breath is when we fill all the way down into our belly, into our chest, and up the back of our throat.

When I am leading guided meditations or teaching others how to meditate, I love to use this visualization: Imagine there is a balloon inside your belly, and as you inhale slowly, you're filling up that balloon. When your balloon is full, continue to hold that beautiful life force energy within your body. As you slowly exhale through your mouth, imagine pulling your belly button to your spine, releasing all that is no longer serving you.

When you first placed your hands on your chest and your belly, were you only breathing into the depths of your chest? Now having the awareness of what a full belly breath feels like, I challenge you to observe your casual breathing as you go about the day. Just adapting the intention of breathing fully into your belly more each day can dramatically reduce stress and quickly aid in regaining a grounded connection within your body.

Other ways to explore how you prefer to recharge:

- Reading for fun
- Taking a nap
- Technology detox
- Go for a walk
- Spend some time in nature
- Cook a nourishing meal
- Give yourself a break from caffeine

As you explore which ways you prefer to recharge, I encourage you to examine the intention behind each action. If you are choosing an option like retail therapy or going out for drinks, what is the real intention your body is trying to communicate to you? Are you choosing to escape rather than rest? Are you uncomfortable being alone with yourself, so you opt for social gatherings? Are you being avoidant in some other area of your life?

Physical Health:

The most common solutions we hear relating to our physical body are diet and exercise. I believe my physical health is so much more than that. The vitality and health of our physiology directly affect everything in our lives, and our physical body is also our energetic body. We store energy in our bodies from past lovers, physical and emotional traumas, our past lives, and the lineage of our families.

In Reiki, we are taught that we can heal seven generations forward and seven generations back. That means that any trauma our ancestors experienced is stored energetically in our lineage until someone chooses to heal it. Having made the vow to heal the lineage of my ancestors and to my future lineage by doing the work now, so to say that the self-care of my physical health is vitally important to me would still be an understatement.

I will be the first to admit that it took a bold experience for me to become willing to get serious about the food I put in my mouth. I will openly admit that I let myself go after my dad passed away unexpectedly in 2020. When he was diagnosed with a rare type of blood cancer, I frightfully learned that this disease could be hereditary. I wallowed in my misery and carbohydrates for a while and then got uncomfortable enough to order some lab work. While this disease is only officially confirmed with a spinal tap, I was now very well versed in the lab markers that are affected once you have this disease. I made the decision that I was going to have these labs done as beginning bench-markers so I could responsibly monitor my health in the years to come.

As the lab results arrived, I was slapped with a rude awakening. My beginning benchmarks were already not great. I again wallowed in my self-pity for a little while, but this time immediately began a diet change. I eliminated all sugar, gluten, processed foods, dairy, and all animal protein except fish. Just like with my addiction, I know myself well enough to know that if I commit to something as a "diet" I will never stick to it, I need to commit to a lifestyle change. I had eliminated coffee from my life a few months prior, so thankfully I had already experienced that detox. At that point in my life, I was seven and a half years clean and sober, and I can honestly say that the most gnarly detoxes that I have experienced were nicotine and sugar!

After about thirty days of my fully committed lifestyle, I began seeing specialist after specialist, each with a different opinion of what could be wrong with me. The funny thing is that none of them have been able to pinpoint any specific autoimmune disease or anything else they thought I had. They just wanted to prescribe me medications and see me again in a few months. I am not one to willingly just accept medication as a Band-Aid or to blindly treat my symptoms just because a doctor tells me to.

A couple of days before my last specialty lab review, my guides came to me again in my dreams. They told me that western medicine was not going to find anything wrong with me and that it was my job alone to use my tools and heal my body in the ways I believe and know how to. They also told me that everything I have been feeling isn't all mine. It is still part of my purpose in this lifetime to heal my lineage.

I woke up the next morning clear that there was not going to be anything definitively diagnosed at the upcoming specialist review appointment, and that I did indeed have all the tools that I needed to heal. As the specialist confirmed all tests were negative, they still suggested three medications to treat my symptoms. I graciously declined because I had already received the confirmation that I had needed. My guides were right, and as I hung up the video conference with the doctor, I firmly decided that I am healing my body, my mind, and my lineage with tools that I know and believe in.

Today, I eat foods as close to their life force energy as I can buy, I move my body regularly, and I am not available for anything that tells me to take a pharmaceutical pill just to mask a symptom. If this feels deeply triggering to you, fantastic! That means that I have struck a chord that your soul is begging you to examine. As always, I am in no way saying this is the only way to believe, but what I am saying is that we all have free will to choose a different path. You are under no obligation to agree with your doctor. You are under no obligation to agree with your parents. You are under no obligation to agree with your president. You have free will to make your own choices. I will repeat that; *you have free will to make your own choices!*

My favorite forms of self-care for my physical health are to:

- Move my body (walk, hike, swim, dance)
- Move my energy (breathwork, Reiki, acupuncture, shaking my ass!)
- Be intentional about what I put in my mouth
- Be intentional about what I put on my skin/body
- Remove, or significantly decrease caffeine
- Remove alcohol, sugar, and other synthetic or processed foods
- Drink all the water!

It's incredible how well your body operates when you feed it nourishing food and drink the appropriate amount of water. I used to *hate* drinking water, but now I can immediately feel the difference between the days when I drink enough water and the days when I do not. I highly recommend getting yourself a water bottle that is large enough to contain your entire day's allotment of water, so you're always very clear on how much more water you have to drink throughout the day. Again, awareness and intention.

I also suggest drinking a full glass of water first thing in the morning, yes, before coffee, to jumpstart your day. I have seen a direct correlation in my ability to drink all of my water for the day if I have a full glass before breakfast or not. It's like that one glass can make or break the day, or I have such a small bladder that I can't drink that much at night, either way... it works for me! If you're not down for carrying around a giant jug of water all day, use it as a benchmark and pour from it into your favorite cup or bottle multiple times throughout the day. Whatever system works best for you, drink yo damn water!

Spiritual Health:

The next bucket of self-care is spiritual health. Spirituality is not religion. Spirituality is an incredibly personal experience for each, and every one of us. Here is my definition of spirituality:

Spirituality is the connection to oneself; one's present self, one's past self, and one's higher self. Spirituality is the connection to one's ancestors. Spirituality is the connection to Mother Earth. Spirituality is one's energetic being connected to all the infinite energy of the universe. Spirituality is a connection with a power greater than oneself, whether that be Source, the Universe, a God of your own understanding, the ocean, or a Mickey Mouse phone. Spirituality is remembering and reconnecting to the light inside of us.

There are infinite variations of spirituality, and I am here to confirm one thing for you: whatever your version of spirituality is right now, is perfect. It will also likely change a hundred more times. That is the beautiful thing about a concept with no rules, there *are* no rules. You can change your mind, adapt, evolve, and grow as many times as you'd like.

Religion can be part of spirituality, but religion is not spirituality. This was a concept that kept me from my spiritual connection for a very long time. I did not identify with any organized religion enough to devote myself entirely to it, so I grew up feeling very alone and confused. I always believed in the universe and evolution, but a lot of my core beliefs did not fit inside any box of organized religion.

This is gravely important for those who grew up with a punishing God or swore off religion forever because of the experiences they had growing up. If this resonates with you, I encourage you to spend some time exploring this section and to ask yourself if you are willing to open your heart up to the vastness of love that is available to you at all times. Just because you may have closed the door on religion does not mean that spirituality is not available to you. The infinite love and abundance of the universe are available to every one of us because it is. It is our birthright, our soul's gift for incarnating on this planet at this time. You are worthy of infinite love and abundance because you are.

Spiritual self-care is any practice of reconnecting with oneself. Spiritual self-care can be any combination of the following practices, but is not limited to this very short list:

- Meditation
- Prayer

- Divination
- Being in nature
- Journaling
- Chanting / Mantra
- Reiki
- Metaphysical Tools
- Religion
- Yoga
- Surfing
- Reading

Personally, my current spiritual practice regularly consists of prayer, meditation, my 12 Step program, self-Reiki, and my daily readers. I have a very active divination practice that consists of oracle + tarot cards, crystals, and channeled writing. I feel the most connected to my higher power when I am at the beach, but any dose of nature will do.

Being sensitive to the energies around me, I am very intentional about regularly clearing and protecting my energy. I regularly excuse myself from "city life" and reconnect with nature for a spiritual reboot. I am very clear that I am not meant to be in one place for too long, and I feel the most energized when I allow myself to interact with new environments. I love to adventure and road trip alone and have been known to book a flight abroad on a random Tuesday and fly someplace I've never been. Traveling alone is one of my very favorite spiritual pastimes.

I have also recently taken up surfing, which has quickly become one of the most spiritual experiences of my life. There is something so magical about being out in the ocean, completely surrendered to her power, and just flowing absolutely in her pulse. The water is cleansing and grounding, and a vast mystery that I may never fully understand. When I need to get right-sized, I immediately drive to the ocean. Whether I just sit on the beach with my toes in the sand, or I'm diving through her waves like a dolphin, she is a power much greater than myself. I am reminded of my temporary place on this earth, and my infinite connection to all the energies of the universe. The noise of the world falls quiet, and I immediately can connect back to myself.

Whether you have an existing spiritual practice or are just learning how important it is to have one, I kindly remind you to begin wherever you are. There is no right or wrong way to develop a spiritual practice, but I lovingly encourage you to find one. Spiritual self-care is the kindest, most gentle, and loving form of self-love one can gift to themselves. Allow it to begin with whatever resonates with you and ask the universe what else is most of your highest good. The answers will come if you ask.

There is a beautiful mantra that I would like to end this section with. That saying is Namaste. Namaste simply and perfectly means that the light in me recognizes and honors the light in you. Because you have listened to the call to pick up this book, I trust that your higher self has guided you here, and to that, I say "Namaste my friend, Namaste."

The Fuck It Bucket:

The next bucket of self-care is called The Fuck It Bucket. This is where you put all of your wildest dreams and greatest desires. These are the bucket list items, and the things that you may only do once in a lifetime. If you have never written a bucket list, I am *so* excited to introduce you to The Fuck It Bucket. I would like for you to take a moment, yes, right now, and write out a list of things to immediately throw in your Fuck It Bucket.

Here are some examples to get you started:

- Skydiving
- Start a business
- Sell a business
- Get married
- Have children
- Hike the Grand Canyon
- Visit the Seven Wonders of the World
- Travel to a foreign country by yourself
- Swim with sharks
- Take salsa dancing lessons
- Ride a horse
- Live in New York City once
- Camp under the Northern Lights

I hope some of these ideas got your wheels turning! If you didn't start writing, seriously stop reading and brain dump everything you can think of right now.

I hope that got your heart racing with ideas for your Fuck It Bucket! This may seem like an extreme category to have present in the conversation of self-care, but I assure you it is not. It is so important to have goals and ambitions to be working toward, but so often that only extends to our work and careers. Having a Fuck It Bucket allows us to have that much-needed sense of adventure and excitement that will ensure that our lives do not become too stagnant in living someone else's version of what our life should be.

As with all the other buckets of self-care, this is personal and customizable to each person. No two Fuck It Buckets will be alike. A person who is an adrenaline junkie will have a very different Fuck It

Bucket than someone who is more timid or conservative. Neither is wrong, and both are correct. I hope that you will continue to grow your list, and most importantly begin to cross it off!

Here are some of my personal Fuck It Bucket examples:

- In 2019, shortly after leaving my companies, I pulled a card from a Sacred Places of the World Oracle card deck. The card was for The Tarkine Rainforest in Tasmania. That week, I booked a flight to Australia and a six-day camping excursion through the Tarkine Rainforest. I didn't tell my friends that I had never been camping before and it was an adventure of a lifetime!
- After spreading my dad's ashes in Arizona, rather than taking either of the usual ways home to California, I drove north to Horseshoe Bend and Zion to reconnect alone with nature.
- I've eaten lamb brain and testicles.
- I've spent weeks in foreign countries alone.
- I've lived bicoastally because I wanted the city and the beach.
- I've experimented with spiritual experiences that scared the shit out of me.
- I got sober (major fuck it bucket experience that was not part of my plan!)
- I've created + built many successful businesses
- I've gotten lots of tattoos
- I've dyed my hair purple
- I've driven across the country (a few times actually)
- When I couldn't decide where to live in SoCal, I moved to Portland to try out the Pacific Northwest for a change
- I've gone on a cruise
- I've learned to surf

Some examples of adventures still in my Fuck It Bucket:

- Go skydiving
- Get married
- Live abroad
- Publish a book (if you're reading this, I've done it. YAY!)
- Become a New York Times Best Selling Author
- Scuba dive
- Swim the Great Barrier Reef
- Lay underneath the Northern Lights
- Visit the village in Greece that my family is from
- Create + publish an Oracle Card deck
- Night surf under a Full Moon

Variety is the spice of life and having a Fuck It Bucket (and using it) connects us back with our childlike sense of wonder and play. This isn't just a feel-good bonus in life, this sense of play and adventure is necessary for our self-care.

Self-Pleasure:

The last section of self-care that I would like to mention is self-pleasure. This conversation may make you deeply uncomfortable, and I am totally okay with that. As always, take what you like and leave the rest, but this is one of my favorite topics to talk and teach about. Self-pleasure is not just throwing on some porn and masturbating to blow off steam at the end of the day. The advent of modern pornography has deeply damaged our sense of self-pleasure and sexual education. There are entire generations now that have grown up with instant access to online pornography and accepted it to be reality, carrying forward that as the expectation of what sex should be.

Self-pleasure is not using someone else to get yourself off or fucking away your feelings. Self-pleasure is connecting with your body and exploring what your body finds safe and inviting. Our bodies hold onto sexual trauma, as well as the energetic exchange between every sexual partner we have had until we release it.

The advent of online dating apps has also created such a disservice to divine energetic connection. Connections are made purely on sexual energy, drawn by the polarity of our own sexual energetic frequencies. We call in what we are. If you are experiencing the same relationship over and over, then that is a pattern within you that is attempting to draw your attention to heal. Until we do the work within ourselves to heal our wounded masculine and feminine traumas, we will continue to call in the same partners over and over. We will forever be stuck in our lower three chakras.

Self-pleasure for self-care is the act of honoring and connecting with your body in safe and sensual ways. That can be in the form of self-massage, masturbating, a soothing bubble bath, dancing, singing, or creating - it all comes from the same energy centers in our bodies. One of my favorite forms of self-pleasure is connecting with my crystal sex toys. Crystals have incredible healing properties and, when used in a practice of sexual pleasure, can be deeply healing. (Important note: Only use crystals specifically and intentionally created for sexual use)

I write this book from the physical form of someone with a vulva and can only speak from that experience. If that does not apply to you, please take the general points and have no attachment to the specifics that I outline. I also am humbly aware that many other identifiers can be used to be inclusive in this conversation, and I choose the words I use to the best of my knowledge and ability at this moment today. Should I be informed of more proper avenues to have this conversation, I am more than willing to learn and to constantly be better. With that said, this is a self-pleasure practice that I regularly share with other vulva owners:

> *Using an ethically sourced crystal sex toy, I lay nude on my back and bring the toy to my heart. I connect deeply with my breath and into my body. I invite the energy of the crystal to connect with me and share this experience with me, only in ways of my highest good. I begin to softly massage my body with the crystal toy. I continue to breathe into the safety of my body as I caress my skin. As I trace the crystal down the inseam of my hips I connect with my body, inquiring if the energy of my toy and the energy of my body feel safe to enter.*
>
> *If my body is relaxed, acknowledges its safety and connection, then I will be inviting and certain inside my soul. My intentions will be clear that this time is for self-pleasure and healing for my highest good. As I caress the areas near my inner thighs, my vulva will invite in the crystal. It will not be forced, and it will naturally flow. As I connect with the crystal within me, I will surrender deeper into my breath and my body. I will allow the toy to move and heal me, and I will let go even deeper with every breath and every orgasm.*

Until I learned to connect with my body in this way, I was constantly attracting sexual partners with unhealed traumas themselves. Connecting with my body in this sensual and safe way has allowed me to open my spiritual, creative, and sexual desires on a whole other level. Today, I am not willing to allow anyone into my intimate space that is not vibrating on a similar frequency. I am only available for high vibe energy and solar system shaking orgasms. I have no shame in saying that some of the best sex I have ever had is with myself!

I am deeply passionate about shattering the walls of self-pleasure conversations and have found after many years of working with private clients and being the go-to sexual consultant for my friends, that *so* many of us want to speak about our sexual energy and self-pleasure questions but have not been taught to have a safe space to do so. Even as I write this book, topics of sexual education, self-pleasure, pornography, and masturbation are all incredibly taboo. I am here to break the ice.

Here are some other forms of self-pleasure as self-care:

- Massage
- Intentional Skin Care
- Breathwork
- Baths
- Swimming
- Dancing
- Walking barefoot in nature
- Sipping tea at sunrise
- Painting, or any other form of creativity

In summary, this ain't your mama's self-care! Self-care is an embodiment of all things for our highest good. Now, go forth and love yo-self.

31

The Commitment to Mastery

Whether in completing my Reiki Master certification, completing Tony Robbins' Mastery University, or stepping into my truth as a spiritual teacher, one thing is for certain - this unraveling is a journey, not a destination. This work is a lifelong commitment to constant and never-ending improvement. It is a commitment to never settling for the status quo, challenging everything, and becoming crystal clear on who we are and what we stand for.

Some days, my truth feels clear as mud, and on other days I am the queen of the world slaying all the limiting beliefs and owning my badge as a Boss Ass Bitch! Both, and everything in between, are all perfect. The goal of Mastery is not perfection. It never has been and never will be. There is no one perfect way, no right way, no holy divine way. There is only one way that resonates with you, at this moment, right now. Only as you process through this moment, will you become available for the next moments.

If anyone crosses your path with *the way* to success, enlightenment, happiness, or fulfillment, wish them well and continue with your bad self - because you already know that not another person on this planet arrived here with the same curriculum for your earth school journey.

Before I send you on your way, back into this big, beautiful world with your newfound awareness and badassery, I want to offer you a couple of final nuggets. As you evolve to every next layer of consciousness, please know that you are shedding a long lineage connected to the pain, trauma, or belief that you just healed. While it may not look and feel like other experiences of grief, you may have encountered thus far on your journey, that periods of grieving may occur.

Should you be met with any deep feelings of loss after a major elevation, please honor the tremendous feat that you have just overcome. Honor your lineage and ancestors that came before you. Honor your parents and guardians in this lifetime who have played their soul agreement out perfectly for you to arrive at this moment of healing. Lastly, please honor yourself for being courageous enough to do this work. I see you and deeply honor you.

As you continue on this journey of self-mastery, you may grow frustrated that you did some questionable things in your life. This path of constant and never-ending improvement also requires an absolute commitment to self-forgiveness. We cannot move forward and properly do this work if we are still carrying around all the stones of pain and misery in our backpacks. Take off your backpack, lay down the stones, and thank them for being part of your journey. It took every single one of those stones for you to arrive at this place today, so honor them, thank them, and for the love of everything that is holy – DO NOT PICK THEM BACK UP AGAIN. This is your eternal permission slip: You are forgiven.

As you go forth and conquer, life will continue to happen. Your old archaic brain will try to go back to doing its job of protecting you and sending in those victim mentalities. However, you now have the awareness that victimhood is just your ego disguised as a bratty little toddler. Lovingly tell your brain to fuck off, you've got it from here. You know that this life is happening for you, not to you.

4

Lessons to Get You Started

If you feel called to "do the work" but do not know where to begin, here are a few of my favorite lessons that I love to share. Perhaps something here will resonate with you. Additional courses and guided meditations can be found at www.morganchonis.com.

- Boundaries
- Learn to Listen
- Overcoming Limiting Beliefs
- How to Stop Self-Sabotage

32

Boundaries

The act of having boundaries means that one is clear about their values and beliefs, and is willing to stand in their truth, even when others do not agree. It is the act of actively choosing to honor oneself. Choosing to stand in one's truth or desire, even in the presence of bullying, is the act of having boundaries.

Learning to have boundaries can be very uncomfortable, but until we can stand firm for what we believe in and desire, we will never truly be in alignment with our divine higher selves.

How to know if you have strong boundaries:

- Do you avoid confrontation?
- Are you easily manipulated?
- Have you fallen victim to gaslighting[8]?
- Is your opinion easily swayed by the opinions of others?
- Do you concern yourself with what others think?
- Do you often consult others before making decisions?
- Do you seek validation from others about the choices you make?
- Can the popular opinion of a group sway you if it differs from yours?
- Do you often feel guilty when disappointing someone?

If you answered yes to any of these questions, then you have opportunities to improve your boundaries. If you are not clear on how to have stronger boundaries, then the work lies in determining your values and desires. Until you are clear on who you are, and what you want, then you cannot stand firmly for yourself.

Personal Example:

I gained clarity along my personal development journey that in order for me to fully be in my zone of genius and be of maximum service to others I need to have my own space to create and recharge. I cannot be around other people as much as others can. I need to have my own private space to retreat to.

For many years, this manifested in long-distance relationships. This worked out well for me because when I was with my partner, I could be present and available for our time together, and when I was alone, I was able to do what I needed to do, as I saw fit. I had my own space to retreat to, and my partner had theirs. This worked out swimmingly until I fell in love with a man and considered settling down and living together.

I was very clear on my needs, we either needed a home with a room that could be my office, or I would rent from a co-working space nearby. I was available for either option but working and having a private practice from home meant I needed a space where I could close the door from the rest of the house. We decided on a beautiful apartment that ticked all the boxes and was head over heels in love.

Within the first month of living together, it painfully came to light that my boundaries were not going to be respected and honored. This boundary of private space was nonnegotiable for me. I took the advice of my married friends and went through many phases of compromise until I was so far out of alignment with my true self that I had to call it off with him. This was a man that I loved deeply, hoped to have children with and marry very soon, but this boundary could not be respected, so I had a choice - Do I stay and waiver my desires for someone else's comfort, or do I stand in my truth for what I need and walk away?

I walked away. That is honoring my boundaries.

Personal Example:

For me, my hometown is like quicksand. It is not my favorite place to be, but I have a lot of history and wonderful people who live there. Over the years, I have learned that I have a three-to-four-day limit before I start itching to leave. If I do not have a defined exit strategy, it is very easy for me to have more people to see, more food to eat, and more things + stuff to do. It is very easy for me to get sucked into its vortex and not leave.

When my dad got diagnosed with Multiple Myeloma and called me to come and help him get his affairs in order, I intended to stay for two weeks. We were just beginning state lockdowns due to Coronavirus, and I decided to spend my two-week quarantine in Tucson with my family. My father's health declined immediately and rapidly, and I adjusted my plans to stay and be with him. He was gone just thirty days after being diagnosed. My choice to stay honored my wishes to be present with my family.

After my dad passed away, I felt responsible for helping my mother understand all of the affairs. After all, I was the one who had sat alone with him on his hospital bed and wrote down everything we needed to know. I knew there were things about the restaurant that my mom and brother hadn't experienced yet, and I would help get them up to speed, then it was ultimately up to my mom what to do with it. She decided to quit her job and commit to running the restaurant.

The laundry list of tasks to get done and affairs to get in order grew longer every day. Three months later, I came up for air for the first time and realized that it had happened again. I had been sucked into the vortex of my hometown, feeling obligated to save the family business. Having been in this situation once before, I knew the familiar signs I was feeling in my body. I booked myself a cabin in the woods for the weekend to get some think-time to myself, and even before getting completely out of town, I knew what I needed to do.

I came to the realization, with trusted counsel and therapy, that I had to arrive at a place where I was comfortable leaving even if it were going to all burst into flames at my departure, and not turn around to come back and save it before I could leave in a healthy fashion. I thought long and hard about what I was and wasn't willing to do before I departed, and I drafted a thirty-day transition plan. I outlined clearly and specifically what I was willing to do, and when I would be departing. I informed my family and staff, and we got to work.

On the day of my intended departure, against the pleas of those around me, I got in my car and drove away. I cried all the way to the freeway, and as I sat at the light before the on-ramp, I asked myself one simple question: "Am I willing to come rushing back if it all goes up in flames?" I took a deep breath and softly answered no. The light turned green, and I went home.

Every single action and decision is always my choice and responsibility. That does not mean that I am honoring myself and my boundaries with each choice. I could blame a million different reasons for that experience, but I actively choose to remove myself from victimhood mindsets. I made the choices that I made and ultimately got uncomfortable enough to hear my body yelling for my attention. I got some space to think, got clear on my values and desires, and set my boundaries. I informed those around me, and I stuck to my decisions.

Did driving away that time hurt like hell? Yes. Was it worth it to stand firm in my boundaries and not allow outside influences to dictate my actions and my feelings? Fuck yeah, it was!

Practicing having boundaries is just that, a practice. One does not automatically or immediately become good at having strong boundaries. Sometimes we will succeed gracefully, other times we will be surprisingly influenced and manipulated. The point is to not beat yourself up along the way and to just keep practicing. As we begin to stand stronger in our boundaries, the more others will respect and honor us in return. It all begins with us.

33

Learn to Listen

In conversation, I will often ask my clients to check in with their bodies. But what does that actually mean, to "check-in with your body"? Our soul communicates with us by way of our emotions, our physical body, and our energetic body.

Have you ever had the experience where the hairs on the back of your neck stood up, and you got the heebie-jeebies about a person or situation who was sketchy? Have you ever been so excited about something that you swear you could just pee your pants? Have you ever just known in your gut that something wasn't right? Have you ever been instantly red zone angry, seemingly out of nowhere?

All of these are examples of your body communicating with you. Our body is always communicating with us, but we are often too busy worrying about other people's opinions, or the incessant noise of our lives to pay attention.

I know that when I am out of alignment, my body will produce anger. I know that when I get edgy for no reason, it's likely because I am hungry and very thirsty. I also know that when I get giddy that I am on to something good. I know that when I feel the pull to retreat to alone time, I better find a way to have some time to myself to recharge my batteries or I am a short fuse away from restless, irritable, and discontent. I know that if I am not asleep before 10:30

p.m., that my body will soon reset, and my creative juices will run wild very shortly thereafter and sleep will be near impossible.

I know my sexual yes. I know my sexual no. I know my energetic safety tells. I know when I have been hooked by an energetic vampire. I know when I am safe to proceed with courage. I know when I am to retreat from danger. I know when my ego is talking, and when my guides or higher self are talking.

People often ask me, "How do I check in with my body to know the right decisions to make?" Here are the two most simple ways to begin:

1. What brings you the most joy? Do that.
2. Is it a full body fuck, yes? If not, then it's a no.

As we begin to pay more attention to our bodies, we will be amazed at what we can learn. One of the greatest things I have ever heard is that "fear is excitement without the breath," by Frederick 'Fritz' Perls, MD. Fear and excitement could not be more opposite emotions, but we can feel them both in our bodies with the subtle difference of a full or shallow breath. Our bodies are truly remarkable communicators when we begin to listen.

In order to listen, we have to slow down. In order to slow down, we have to breathe. In order to breathe, we have to exhale completely and fully before we can inhale. In the same moment, we can feel fear about a situation, we can then realize that we are only breathing shallowly into our chest and be instantly transformed into excitement after a couple of full belly deep breaths.

Our bodies will use whatever means necessary to get our attention. If we are not embodying excitement in a joyful moment, we may become short of breath, anxious, and fearful. That fear is nudging us to slow down and reconnect with our bodies. As we've just outlined, when we slow down and breathe, the real emotion is excitement, not fear.

I can summarize what my body has taught me in a few simple statements:

1. The path to fulfillment is to follow the joy.
2. Creative energy and sexual energy often feel like the same thing.
3. Anger, frustration, resentment, physical aches + pains, and dis-ease are all physical manifestations of being out of alignment.
4. If I do not listen to the subtle communications from my body, she will get louder and more abrasive until I am so uncomfortable that I cannot help but pay attention.

34

Overcoming Limiting Beliefs

Over the last eighteen months, I have been deep diving into my greatest fears and limiting beliefs, rewriting my truths, and reprogramming my mind. As I listened to one of my mentor's voices one morning, I heard an inner knowing and pulled out my phone to send myself a text message, my go-to way to make a note when I'm on the move. The text message read: "What is my issue with calling myself a Life Coach?"

In my personal development with my own coaches and my astrologer, I've processed through a lot of shadow work around the notion of identity. I have studied the work of Ram Dass, and other spiritual teachers, diving into the goal of Becoming Nobody. Labels and other societal identifiers are conditioned pillars of importance and significance. I'm deep enough into this journey to understand these identifiers do not control my self-worth, but wise enough to know that the more I learn the more I have to learn.

I've been told by social media experts of the importance of my Instagram bio. I have a note on my phone of every version of this important business tool that I have evolved through over the years. Since going "all in" on myself and my new business endeavors I have struggled with what to call myself and what to say when people ask me what I do.

I know that I don't have any desire to fit into most boxes. I know the disdain I feel with labels and expectations, yet there is a tiny voice in the back of my mind that says, "that's all well and good Morgan, but you still have to do it." Ugh. The bane of my existence as a Human Design Manifestor[9] is being told what I "should do," and "how to be successful." When I check in with my body about what my truth is, that is *not* the way to influence me into action! That is, however, the fast track to meeting my resistance and ultimately the anger of my sharp tongue. I hate the pressure that I feel to describe myself in one hundred and fifty words or less.

One of my favorite meditative practices is to go for a drive. The windshield time allows me to have something to focus on, driving safely, while allowing my brain to loosely wander. One of the most confusing spiritual guidelines I had ever heard was the phrase "hold on loosely." "What the actual fuck does that mean?!" my analytical, ego-driven thoughts originally declared. I understand this now when I go for a drive.

If I have something on my mind or a problem to work through, or if I'm seeking inspiration, the windshield time allows me the space to float. I can get out of my head and into a flow. Another way that I love to get into a flow state is what I like to call "word vomit," a form of freewriting with no intention - just write and see what pours out. Both word vomit writing and unattached windshield time allow me to connect to my higher self without overanalyzing. On this particular day, the inspired action was to get out of my house and go for a drive.

I wound up at one of my favorite local spots where I ordered some food to take to the park. Unattached to what the day would bring, I brought all of the things with me to the park: a blanket, one of the books I am reading, my computer, my notebook, a delicious beverage, some snacks, you know... the essentials!

While waiting for my food, I pulled out the notes section on my phone, which is how I begin most word vomit sessions. The only intention I was loosely holding was the text message that I sent to myself, "What is my issue with calling myself a Life Coach?" I prayed to surrender to creative solutions and began to type.

As my food arrived, I headed to the park with all of my essentials for an unattached day. It was a perfect day at the park, there was a light breeze, the sun was out, plenty of trees to choose from for a shady post. First, I always remove my shoes. My flip-flops flew off my feet and my toes breathed in the moisture of the grass between my toes.

Then I lay down my backpack, spread out my blanket, and melted into the perfect seventy-five-degree Southern California day. As I had a few bites of my food, the words screamed to pour out of me. So I pulled out my laptop, opened my note from the coffee shop, and found myself back at my word vomit of "What is my issue with calling myself a Life Coach?"

As I stared off at the butterflies playing in the background, the words, "How would I advise a client?" spoke through me. Sometimes I get so caught up in the noise in my head that I forget overcoming fears and limiting beliefs is such a simple process. Instead of allowing myself to hold onto this discomfort for one more day, I was going to take myself through the same process I would with a client.

Before this moment, I had never written this process down but rather allowed it to be channeled through me in the appropriate moments when needed. I didn't feel any resistance to doing this work at that moment because the communications had been so clear to me all day.

I was willing to turn the lens on myself and see where we landed. I say we because I understand that this is not solely my doing. This is part of the co-creation with the universe, and I am merely a conduit for these words to emerge through me. So, here we go...

Step One: What do I currently believe?
Do not filter myself, judge myself, or sensor myself. Just word vomit. Go!

- I have a big resistance to calling myself a Life Coach.
- Why do I feel that way?
    - There is a ton of negative connotations about Life Coaching as a profession.
    - They are not taken as seriously as a medical professional
    - It is not a regulated field, so there are a ton of people out there doing really shitty work.
    - The Self Knowledge industry is booming, there are a ton of people taking advantage of an up-and-coming field - delivering really shitty work.
    - I will be judged
    - I will not be taken seriously
    - People will not see the value in my work
    - People will not think I am qualified
    - I am concerned about the words on my business card or Instagram bio over my why.

Step Two: Do I believe this is a limiting belief?
For each point written, assess the statement. What I mean here is:
Do I believe this belief is a load of horse shit?
Do I believe that this belief is causing me harm?
Do I feel aligned with this statement?
Does it make me feel good?

Going back over my list...

- I have a big resistance to calling myself a Life Coach.
  - Yes, this is a limiting belief.
- Why do I feel that way?
  - I have not done the work to remove this block. It is causing harm to my self-worth for the work that I am doing with people.
- There are a ton of negative connotations about Life Coaching as a profession.
  - Yes, this is a limiting belief.
- They are not taken as seriously as a medical professional
  - Yes, this is a limiting belief.
- It is not a regulated field, so there are a ton of people out there doing really shitty work.
  - Yes, this is a limiting belief.
- The Self Knowledge industry is booming, there are a ton of people taking advantage of an up-and-coming field - delivering really shitty work.
  - Yes, this is a limiting belief.
- I will be judged
  - Yes, this is a limiting belief.
- I will not be taken seriously
  - Yes, this is a limiting belief.
- People will not see the value in my work
  - Yes, this is a limiting belief.
- People will not think I am qualified
  - Yes, this is a limiting belief.
- I am concerned about the words on my business card or Instagram bio over my "why".
  - Yes, this is a limiting belief.

<u>Step Three: Am I willing to see things differently?</u>
For each statement, ask myself "am I willing to see things differently?"

I don't need to know how to fix anything at this point, I am just assessing if I even have the willingness to see things differently. This is a simple yes or no question. If the answer is no, I am not willing to see things differently, then I can stop here and go on my merry way being closed-minded, miserable, and discontent. If I answer yes, I am indeed willing to see things differently, then I have now granted myself a tiny window of hope.

This window only needs to be a tiny crack to keep moving forward. Having a willingness to see things differently gives me the crack I need to make a change. Answering no keeps me in a fortress of concrete walls of certainty, which keeps me spiraling in self-pity, irritability, overanalyzing repetitive pain and misery. I only need a crack to break free. I only have to be WILLING to see things differently.

Going back over my list...

- I have a big resistance to calling myself a Life Coach.
  - Yes, this is a limiting belief.
  - Yes, I am willing to see things differently.
- Why do I feel that way?
  - I have not done the work to remove this block. It is causing harm to my self-worth for the work that I am doing with people.
  - Yes, I am willing to see things differently.
- There are a ton of negative connotations about Life Coaching as a profession.

- ◦ Yes, this is a limiting belief.
- ◦ Yes, I am willing to see things differently.
- ◦ They are not taken as seriously as a medical professional
  - ◦ Yes, this is a limiting belief.
  - ◦ Yes, I am willing to see things differently.
- ◦ It is not a regulated field, so there are a ton of people out there doing really shitty work.
  - ◦ Yes, this is a limiting belief.
  - ◦ Yes, I am willing to see things differently.
- ◦ The Self Knowledge industry is booming, there are a ton of people taking advantage of an up-and-coming field - delivering really shitty work.
  - ◦ Yes, this is a limiting belief.
  - ◦ Yes, I am willing to see things differently.
- ◦ I will be judged
  - ◦ Yes, this is a limiting belief.
  - ◦ Yes, I am willing to see things differently.
- ◦ I will not be taken seriously
  - ◦ Yes, this is a limiting belief.
  - ◦ Yes, I am willing to see things differently.
- ◦ People will not see the value in my work
  - ◦ Yes, this is a limiting belief.
  - ◦ Yes, I am willing to see things differently.
- ◦ People will not think I am qualified
  - ◦ Yes, this is a limiting belief.
  - ◦ Yes, I am willing to see things differently.
- ◦ I am concerned about the words on my business card or Instagram bio over my "why"
  - ◦ Yes, this is a limiting belief.
  - ◦ Yes, I am willing to see things differently.

<u>Step Four: Is this ultimately true?</u>
For each point, with the willingness to see things differently, ask myself "is this statement ultimately true?"

- Opinions are like assholes, everyone has one. Are these beliefs ultimately true of me and for me? No.

<u>Step Five: What is ultimately true?</u>
For each point, now seeing that this is ultimately not true, word vomit on what is ultimately true.

- I am not a shitty person taking advantage of people, capitalizing on other's pain and suffering. I am very clear on my highest core values, and I am great at what I do.

  Going back to my list...
- I have a big resistance to calling myself a Life Coach
  - The truth is that I am listening to the opinions of others, mostly people who are not willing to do the work or look honestly within themselves. People who value society's identifiers as determinations of value + status. That is not me.
- Why do I feel that way?
  - I feel this way because I have not allowed myself to work through this belief before today, so OBVI - it is still a limiting belief that I carried.
- There are a ton of negative connotations about Life Coaching as a profession.
  - The work is often challenging the status quo of our society, so of course, those who want us to remain the

same will try to discredit those willing to guide others to the path of bettering themselves.

- They are not taken as seriously as a medical professional
  - Western medicine as a whole, in my opinion, falls into the category of outdated patriarchy, along with other forms of government and big pharma.
  - My goal has NEVER been to be a medical professional by the standard of patriarchal definition. My goal is always only driven by the notion that when we heal ourselves, we heal the world, to heal myself + help others to do the same.
- It is not a regulated field, so there are a ton of people out there doing really shitty work.
  - While there may be people out there doing work that is not in alignment with my core values, it is not my job to take other people's inventory. I have no control over other people, places, or things. I can only control the quality of work that I do, and the authenticity in which I speak.
- The Self Knowledge industry is booming, there are a ton of people taking advantage of an up-and-coming field - delivering really shitty work.
  - Again, just an opinion. The knowledge industry is indeed booming! I believe it is still in its early infant phases and has a very long road of thriving importance. That does not make me a bad person for choosing this work, it is merely an opportunity to reach more people because the industry is becoming more widely understood and accepted. Raising the consciousness of the masses takes time, people are not going to all be willing

to be open-minded to alternative forms of education as quickly as I am.

- ○ I will be judged
    - ○ I am going to be judged *no matter what* I do! So wouldn't it be better to just live my life in alignment for my highest good?? Yup!
- ○ I will not be taken seriously
    - ○ If people don't take me seriously, then those are not my people. Plain + Simple!
- ○ People will not see the value in my work
    - ○ My ideal clients will all find their way to me when they are ready. Those that are not in alignment are not my people. They can move along. By repelling those, I am making room for my ideal clients to find me.
- ○ People will not think I am qualified
    - ○ Again, just an opinion. My integrity speaks from authenticity and experience. I only teach that which I know. I do not share anything that I have not done or been through myself. Because my truth is my own experience, I am always 100% qualified.
- ○ I am concerned about the words on my business card or Instagram bio over my why.
    - ○ That is my ego at work. My ego is not my truth, my truth is birthed from my heart. What is on my business card or written in my IG bio are the tiniest spaces in the entire world to try to explain who I am + what I do. I am such a complex + vibrant being, how could I ever expect 150 words or less to articulate the work perfectly and completely about what it is that I do with people?! Literally *every single day* I am evolving + growing personally and professionally... good luck to anyone who

wants to try and categorize me into a few words. It's exhausting, let me tell you. I don't want to ever spend this much time or energy on it ever again!

Step Six: What is the new story?

Am I willing to carry the old limiting beliefs with me moving forward? If not, what is the new story?

I am no longer willing to carry these limiting beliefs about labeling myself as a Life Coach. My work speaks for itself, based on the feedback from my real-life clients. The value is in the content that I create, not the label I place on it. My worth could never be described in 150 words or less + I don't ever want to put that much energy into trying to do so again. I am constantly evolving + on a path of never-ending improvement. I will never fit into a single box. I am growing every single day, honing my craft, being called into deeper alignment of service all the time, what I call myself is not important. How I show up, the authenticity in which I speak, the compassion in which I create sacred spaces for others; that is what is important. When I take inspired, aligned action, I will always speak for and to those who need me.

Step Seven: Decide with absolute certainty.

Check-in with my body, is the new story a truth that is in alignment with my core values, integrity, and direction I am heading in my life?

If not, what resistance is showing up? What stories am I still telling myself that are holding me back from absolute certainty? Repeat Steps 1-6 for these.

If I answered yes, this new story is in alignment with my highest truth + intention then *whoop! Whoop!* Let the old story blow away in the wind, it's no longer my truth. Only the new story gets to come with me as I go about my day. I am not willing to carry that old story anymore. BYE FELICIA!

Upon completion, I take a deep cleansing breath through my nose. Filing my belly. Filing my chest. Holding at the top. Feeling the perfect breeze on my skin. What is a statement that I know to be true?

"This work is fucking important"

"My work is of high service, and worthy of massive compensation"

My heart flutters!

Exhale.

My name is Morgan Chonis, and I am here to raise the vibration of this planet. I am here to heal myself + teach others to do the same. When we heal ourselves, we heal the world.

35 ▌

How to Stop Self-Sabotage

Here is what I know to be true: our simple human brains do the very best they can to protect us and keep us safe from the proverbial saber-toothed tiger. As evolving spiritual beings, it is our duty to re-program the outdated systems and replace them with more evolved software.

One way that our brains try to protect us is by keeping us in our comfort zones when we are experiencing success. This translates into the physical realm as self-sabotage. Imagine that you are a glass thermometer. And as you become more successful, the thermometer reading increases. Success to you can be defined however you see fit - happiness, love, money, experiences, etc.

Now imagine that as you are achieving more, your thermometer gauge begins to push against the glass ceiling. When you reach the top of your thermometer gauge, it will signal to your brain that you are in danger of running out of space. So your simple human brain will say, "Oh! I can help with this problem!" and proceeds to do whatever it needs to do to bring you back to safety.

Consciously or unconsciously, we become an energetic match for an experience that brings us back to right-sized. Our brains want us to stay small and safe. We can't be attacked by saber-toothed tigers if we are small and safe!

Think about lottery winners. How many times have we not heard stories of people winning millions of dollars, only to go right back to where they started, or even become worse off, within a few years. Think about something great that has happened in your life, then think about what happened to that great thing. It was probably immediately followed by an accident or illness. Think about sharing the exciting news about your promotion with your spouse only to end up in a screaming fight shortly after. These are all examples of self-sabotage.

Self-Sabotage is the thing that happens directly after something positive, causing our temperature gauge to come back down to neutral. It is the self-sabotaging action or thought immediately following your success. You might be thinking this all sounds crazy, but let me ask you a couple of simple questions:

° Do you believe that you have to have the bad to accompany the good?
° Do you believe that we have to have heartache to appreciate the sweet?
° Do you believe that sadness is required to accompany happiness?
° Do you believe that "that's just the way it is sometimes"?
° Do you believe you're just destined to be this way?

Here's the thing about beliefs, they are just thoughts that you have told yourself enough times to believe that they are the truth. What if you could experience success, catch your self-sabotaging behaviors in action, and then choose a different action? Would you do it?

We have talked about overcoming limiting beliefs, but this is next-level shit right here! This is the work that shatters the top off the glass thermometer and allows you to experience good-feeling feelings more often. You can reprogram your brain to stop sending you back to playing small and safe.

Personal Example: This first poem is from the night I committed to writing this book

THE DAY I HIRED MY WRITING COACH
IT IS THE TWENTY-THIRD DAY OF DECEMBER OF THE WEIRDEST
YEAR OF MY LIFE.
IT IS 2020.
IT'S SUDDENLY BLUSTERY AND A CHILL HAS COME OVER ME WHILE
I WALK THE DOG.
I AM HOME FOR CHRISTMAS, AND I CANNOT STOP CRYING.
OF ALL THE TEARS THAT THIS YEAR HAS BESTOWED UPON ME,
THESE ARE SOMEHOW DIFFERENT.

I CAN LOOK MYSELF DEEP IN THE EYE WHEN I WALK BACK INTO
THE HOUSE.
MASCARA PAINTED DOWN MY CHEEKS AS I SEEMINGLY UGLY CRY.
THIS ONE IS DIFFERENT.
THIS ONE IS NOT PAIN.
THIS ONE IS NOT GRIEF.
THIS ONE IS NOT HEARTBREAK.

THIS ONE SAYS, "YES GIRL, YES!"
"THIS IS WHAT IT FEELS LIKE TO TAKE ALIGNED ACTION FOR YOUR
HIGHEST SELF.
"THIS IS PURE JOY + HAPPINESS!"
SO WHY THE HYSTERICAL TEARS?!

I JUST MET MY PERSON.

I JUST HUNG UP A LIFE-CHANGING PHONE CALL.

I JUST HUNG UP THE PHONE WITH THE GUIDE WHO IS GOING TO
USHER ME THROUGH THIS BIRTHING PROCESS.

I JUST HUNG UP WITH A SPIRIT WHO CAST AN ARROW INTO MY
SOUL AND SAID,

"TAKE MY HAND, I WILL TRUDGE THIS ROAD WITH YOU."

I HAVE JUST HUNG UP WITH THE WOMAN WHO HAS JUST AGREED
TO MENTOR ME THROUGH THE SPIRITUAL EXPERIENCE OF MY FIRST
BOOK.

I HAVE JUST HIRED MY WRITING COACH FOR MY VERY FIRST BOOK.

IT IS TIME. THE UNIVERSE HAS SPOKEN.

I AM NO LONGER AVAILABLE TO STAY SMALL.

THIS IS AN UNAPOLOGETIC VOICE + IT IS TIME TO BE HEARD.

This second poem was written exactly one hour later while sitting on the toilet alone in the bathroom bawling my eyes out in sadness:

AND AT THE HEIGHT OF HER EXCITEMENT

PERHAPS THE MOST MEANINGFUL NIGHT OF HER LIFE

SHE FOUND HERSELF STARING PAST THE GLIMMERING FACES

ONLY WITH ONE FACE IN HER VIEW

IT'S TOO BAD YOU COULDN'T BE HERE TO SHARE THE NEWS

IT'S TOO BAD ALL YOU SEEMED TO CARE ABOUT IS YOU

I TURNED TO FIND YOUR HAND + SHARE IN THE EXCITEMENT BUT

WAS STRICKEN BACK TO REALITY

I NEVER EVEN HAD YOU.

I went from the highest high to the lowest low in a matter of one hour. I always knew that I was destined to write. I also always knew that Liam would be there to support me. The desire to pick a fight with Liam or to feel sorry for myself about him not choosing me has always been a common self-sabotaging behavior for me. It's one of my go-to behaviors.

While I was in the heightened energy of my successes, as displayed in my first poem, my brain immediately jumped in to help bring me back down to right-sized. As I sat on the toilet, hysterically crying that Liam wouldn't be here to share this experience with me I caught my self-sabotaging thoughts in action. It dawned on me right there, with snot running down my face!

"THIS IS EXACTLY WHAT I HAVE BEEN LEARNING ABOUT!" I screamed at myself on the toilet. I took a deep breath, and I told my brain "No. Thank You."

In full transparency, I *actually* said, "Fuck you, brain! You're not going to ruin this moment for me! Liam isn't here because Liam chose not to be here, that is *not* my problem. This is my time!" and I wiped the snot off my face and got myself together to respond to the celebratory text messages that were already pouring in. I caught my self-sabotaging problem in action, and I chose a different path.

There has only been one other time since then that thoughts of Liam tried to sabotage my happiness in this journey. I caught it immediately, thanked my Higher Power for helping me get so good at this, and redirected my attention to the cute surfer boy who was placing his jacket over my cold shoulders as we walked down the boardwalk at Seventeenth Street. The self-sabotaging thoughts of Liam no longer have control over my life today. I no longer place him on that god-like pedestal. And when thoughts of him come up, I wish him well with good vibes and infinite happiness.

If you have stuck with me this far in my journey, I know that you are intrigued to experience this type of freedom and happiness too. I know that there is something inside of you that wants to experience this level of pleasure and joy. If you want more, please take this vow with me right now.

I, _____(your name), vow to call out my self-sabotaging behaviors in action, tell them "Thank you, but no thank you," and choose to live in the good-feeling feelings for longer.

Every time you catch a self-sabotaging behavior in action, the distance between you and that glass thermometer increases. You, my friend, are allowed to soar. You deserve to feel better longer. You get to be wildly successful because you do. It is your motherfucking birthright! As Maya Angelou and I like to say, when we know better, we can do better. Please let this awareness sink in. You deserve to live the life of your dreams. You deserve massive happiness because you do.

Every time you catch your brain sending in a self-sabotaging thought, choose to not accept it, and fucking celebrate! I prefer to give myself a high-five or do a one-arm in-the-air superman jump, but whatever celebratory action feels juiciest to you is perfect. Please know I am with you in spirit, cheering you on as you smash your limiting beliefs and self-sabotaging behaviors! Keep me in your pocket and call me the ultimate hype (wo)man. Woo! You got this!

ACKNOWLEDGMENTS

Marm - Thank you for persistently reminding me that my words are my greatest gifts. Thank you for listening to all the signs, all the connections, all the guidance that this is the path. I love you so much and I am so grateful to see your face at every reading, at every event, and that you're the first to share every single thing that I do. Thank you for being the OG Cheerleader!

Papa - Thank you for giving me the gift of my voice. Thank you for being my greatest role model and my very best friend. Thank you for the McGuyver Skills and for always having my back. Thank you for raising a daughter bold enough to make it in a man's world, and gently loving me as I burned it all to the ground. Thank you for being by my side every step of the way. I know you are here with me, and never lost. I will always be that little girl in the polka dot dress pushing you on her bicycle. From the bottom of my heart, I love you.

Dimitri - I love you more than you will ever know.

Staci - Thank you for accepting me, guiding me, and never abandoning me. Pistachio.

To my Kristal - I literally cannot imagine this world without you. Thank you for all of the things. Thank you for loving me through all of the things. Thank you for never judging, and never giving up. I love you; I love you; I love you.

Nicolie - Thank you for finding our family and never letting go. There never have been enough words, and there still aren't enough words. I love you, my soul sister!

To my HB tribe + The Girls - you are all beyond my wildest dreams. Thank you for loving me while I learned to love myself. Thank you for catching me, thank you for holding me, thank you for creating space for all the yuckiest and most wonderful moments of my life. I love each and every one of you to the moon.

Kellie - Thank you for hugging me and never letting go. Thank you for giving me a home when I lost mine. Thank you for showing me that I am a complex human with complex emotions, and how beautiful we get to be. I am so grateful to you.

Liz - Thank god Tony brought us together! Thank you for holding space for me each and every week. You have been the most incredible accountability buddy + friend through this roller coaster of life. I am SOul grateful for you sister!

Carrie - Thank you for taking my hand and illuminating the path to meeting Sarah and birthing this book. Thank you for holding space as I processed through each, and every wave and for believing in me to soar.

Sarah - Thank you for making yourself known and co-creating this book with me. It has been the honor of my life to create such magic with you.

Amma - Thank you for supporting me to take this vulnerable story and polish it into a stunning work of art. You heard my intentions of making sure the magic + energy of my words remained and guided me to a new level of mastery. Thank you for celebrating my bold desires to ruffle some feathers + speak *all* of my truth.

Nick at Costa Mesa Recording Studios - Thank you for taking my vision + supporting me to create another work of art. I am so proud of what we've created together.

To my team in New York - words cannot express how much I respect and love you all. There is an unbreakable bond when we go through the trenches together that way. I hold each and every one of you in the highest regard and cannot express my gratitude enough for the time that we had together. I would not be the woman that I am today without the experiences I shared with each of you. Thank you!

Erica - Thank you for taking a chance on me when it would come to lay the foundation for the rest of my life. Thank you for the adventures, and for the life-changing moments that began over carne asada fries + turkey meatballs! I am so grateful to call you my friend.

Nicolette - Woman, there is no doubt that you were divinely guided into my life. I could not be prouder of the woman that you are today, and I absolutely would not have been able to survive without you by my side. Thank you for believing in me, jumping into my crazy life, and never, ever running when shit got wild. You are a true angel on earth + I LOVE watching you thrive in your own light. Thank you for trusting me and being such a beautiful friend.

Mathey - I can already feel your eyes rolling, but I'm going to tell you anyway. Thank you for being such a wonderful friend to me all of these years. Seriously.

Shaní + Chelsea - Thank you for stepping into my life, my sisters in light. I am so grateful for the work we have created together, and know it is but the beginning. Thank you for believing in me and this mission. You both have been instrumental in birthing this movement. Thank you, thank you, thank you!

Hendo - I am really proud of us!

To all my spiritual teachers, guides + mentors - Thank you for illuminating the light for me to find my way home.

Jamie - Thank you for guiding me on this journey into the light. I am forever grateful for your heart and kindness.

To the men of my stories – Thank you for being my mirrors and my teachers. Thank you for playing your soul agreement so perfectly for me to learn + grow.

To My Cheerleading Support Squad - Holy moly, your energy throughout this book writing process has been invaluable. I was hell-bent on breaking the moody, dramatic archetype of being a writer and you all really showed up for the challenge! I love you + cannot thank you enough.

To you, my reader - I thank you from the bottom of my heart for allowing me to share this sacred experience with you. I hope our paths do cross again, and should you ever need any guidance along your journey, flick on that little light inside you and allow it to guide you. You are always and forever connected to the Great Universal Source because you are. Here's to being wild, radical, and true. Shine on, dear one, shine on. Thank you for following the little nudge of your soul to pick up this book. It has been the honor of my life to create it for you + I hope it is the mirror that you didn't know you needed. I love you and I look forward to meeting you again so very soon! xo - Morgan

1. Transition into the Age of Aquarius: The paradigm shift from the current patriarchy - Age of Pisces: rigid power ruled by few, enslaved by ego - into the Age of Aquarius, or the Light Age. A global consciousness shifting into community, service, collective - lead by Source + Divine Feminine. Power is shifting to the individual, providing freedom of sovereignty of self and alignment with soul.

2. Ayurveda: often considered one of the world's oldest healing systems, Ayurveda is the Hindu wellness practice of holistic whole-body balance of mind, body + spirit.

3. Primary Core Values: Tony Robbins teaches the Six Basic Human needs - Certainty, Variety/Uncertainty, Significance, Love/Connection, Growth, Contribution - as primary drivers for human behaviors.

4. Womxn: a term of gender neutrality to be inclusive of all who may identify as a feminine leading energy - inclusive of all cis, trans + nonbinary individuals.

5. Victim Mindset: The idea that everything is happening to us. Taking no responsibility for the course of action transpiring in our life. Unwilling to see the part we have played.

6. Masculine Patriarchy: The era of society being led by a powerful few over the last few millennia, commonly referred to as the energy of the Wounded Masculine. The wounded mascu-

line energy can be described as controlling, forceful, manipulative, distracted, overcompensating and aggressive.

7. A new pair-a-boots: referring to the saying of using "concrete shoes" as a method of body disposal, usually associated with criminal activity, to ensure that a body sinks to the bottom of the river or ocean.

8. Gaslighting: psychological manipulation intended to change or challenge one's own sanity.

9. Human Design Manifestor: Human Design is a blueprint of your soul that combines the ancient systems of Astrology, the Chinese I 'Ching, The Hindu-Brahmin Chakras and the Tree of Life from the Zohar/Kabbalist tradition, along with contemporary disciplines of Quantum Mechanics, Astronomy, Genetics, and Biochemistry.

REFERENCES

"Becoming Nobody." Gaia. Gaia. Accessed September 12, 2021. https://www.gaia.com/video/becoming-nobody?

Bodin, Luc, Nathalie Bodin Lamboy, Jean Graciet, and Jon E. Graham. *The Book OF Ho'oponopono: The Hawaiian Practice of Forgiveness and Healing*. Rochester, VT: Destiny Books, 2016.

Brittany, and Brianne Liana. "Ram Dass Quotes." Ram Dass, August 14, 2020. https://www.ramdass.org/ram-dass-quotes

Bunnell, Lynda, and Ra Uru Hu. *The Definitive Book of Human Design: The Science of Differentiation*. Carlsbad, CA: HDC Pub., 2012.

Demarco, Stacey. *Earth Power Oracle: An Atlas for the Soul*. U S Games Systems, 2015.

Doran, BS, RMT, Bernadette. "The Science Behind Reiki." *Equilibrium Energy + Education*, 2009. https://www.equilibrium-e3.com/images/PDF/Science%20Behind%20Reiki.pdf

Frances, Amanda. "Coaches: How to Attract Clients: Amanda Frances." amanda frances | business mentor + money queen + spiritual bosslady, November 13, 2019. https://amandafrances.com/the-energy-of-getting-paid-with-ease/.

Hendricks, Gay. *The Big Leap: Conquer Your Hidden Fear and Take Life to the Next Level.* New York: HarperCollins, 2010.

Jung, C. G., and Hull Richard Francis Carrington. *The Philosophical Tree, 335.* London: Routledge and K. Paul, 1967.

Posted by: Team Tony. "6 Human Needs: Why Are They So Important?" tonyrobbins.com, June 29, 2021. https://www.tonyrobbins.com/mind-meaning/do-you-need-to-feel-significant/.

"Reiki Factsheet." *Cleveland Clinic Wellness.* Center for Integrative Medicine for Reiki. https://my.clevelandclinic.org/ccf/media/files/Wellness/reiki-factsheet.pdf.

Reiki News. "Reiki News Summer 2009." Reiki, February 8, 2021. https://www.reiki.org/store/reiki-news-magazine/reiki-news-summer-2009.

Morgan Chonis is an Author, Reiki Master, Meditation Guide + Transformation Coach. As a lifetime seeker, it is her mission as a spiritual teacher to take herself through the deepest healing + training programs required for self-mastery. In doing so, she vulnerably shares her experience, strength + hope with her audience.

Combined with a background in corporate success coaching, Morgan is an expert at initiating transformation, growth, accountability + clarity. Her zone of genius is creating safe, intimate spaces for her students to become raw + honest with their truths. Through understanding our body's communication, mindset training, overcoming fears + limiting beliefs, and reconnecting with their soul - Morgan helps guide her students on the path to their juiciest lives!

She has trained with some of the world's most successful personal development coaches to put together her own flavor of all the best tools. Morgan continues to push the boundaries of her soul in order to be of maximum service to others.

Thriving in the ocean breezes of sunny Southern California, originally from Tucson, Arizona, Morgan now resides wherever the wind takes her.

"I vowed that if I was shown how to smash societal expectations, heal my generational lineage + forge a path all my own, then I would show others how to do the same." - Morgan Chonis

Website: www.morganchonis.com
Instagram: @morganchonis
TikTok: @morganchonis
Facebook: @morganchonishealing
The Vibrate Higher Podcast, available on all streaming platforms.

IN LOVING MEMORY OF MY HERO + BEST FRIEND

CPSIA information can be obtained
at www.ICGtesting.com
Printed in the USA
BVHW051359281021
620179BV00014B/309

9 781737 850205